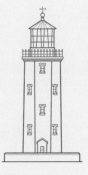

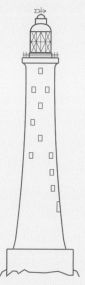

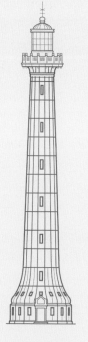

A BRIEF ATLAS OF
THE LIGHTHOUSES AT
THE END OF THE WORLD

A BRIEF

ATLAS

OF THE

LIGHT-
HOUSES

AT THE

END OF THE
WORLD

GONZÁLEZ MACÍAS

TRANSLATED BY DANIEL HAHN

PICADOR

First published 2023 by Picador
an imprint of Pan Macmillan
The Smithson, 6 Briset Street, London EC1M 5NR
EU representative: Macmillan Publishers Ireland Ltd, 1st Floor,
The Liffey Trust Centre, 117–126 Sheriff Street Upper,
Dublin 1, D01 YC43
Associated companies throughout the world
www.panmacmillan.com

ISBN 978-1-5290-8714-7

Originally published 2020 by Ediciones Menguantes, León, Spain. Eighth edition 2022.

9 8 7 6 5 4 3 2 1

A CIP catalogue record for this book is available from the British Library.

Map artwork, illustrations and design by José Luis González Macías.

Printed and bound in Malaysia

Visit www.picador.com to read more about all our books
and to buy them. You will also find features, author interviews and
news of any author events, and you can sign up for e-newsletters
so that you're always first to hear about our new releases.

Contents

Needless to say, the Lighthouse at the End of the World had a fixed light, and there was no fear that the captain of a ship might confuse it with some other, since no other lighthouse existed around those parts.

Jules Verne
The Lighthouse at
the End of the World

A short prologue

When I mentioned, in the course of a family lunch, that I was planning to write a book about lighthouses, my father looked very sceptical and exclaimed: 'Lighthouses? But you're just as much of a landlubber as I am!' He is quite right. I was born in the interior of the Iberian Peninsula, and with the exception of a few short years, I have always lived far from the sea. And so I ought to warn the reader: the man hiding behind these pages is an impostor. Although I did allow myself to be seduced by lighthouses long ago, and I have sometimes felt the pressing need to run off to some Galician or Asturian cape in pursuit of them, as you probably have too, I am sorry to have to report, unfortunately for you, that I am no expert.

For some time, I have felt like creating a book using materials that are everyday to me: texts, drawings, cartography, pictures . . . common elements that just happen to pass through my hands in my day-to-day work. I had an idea going round and round my head, one that I'd inherited from the books I've enjoyed – poetical atlases illustrated with maps and filled with fleeting tales capable of taking us on journeys to distant places from the comfort of our armchair – but I needed a motif to anchor it. If this book about remote lighthouses has found its way into your hands, it's thanks to a couple of chance events. First, I was commissioned to design an album cover for a band called North of South, and instinctively it seemed right to draw dreamlike pictures of a number of lighthouses installed on asteroids floating in the sky and casting light onto outer space. As I did my research to produce the illustrations, a torrent of extraordinary beauty caught my eye. I was gazing at one lighthouse after another and I couldn't stop admiring them. The second reason was my encountering – also on a professional matter – José Luis Viñas's *The Sixth Extinction: An Atlas of Absent Biodiversity*, an artistic project that deals with the disappearance of certain bird species. That was how I came across the story of the *Xenicus lyalli* and the Stephens Island lighthouse, in which every last specimen of a small New Zealand bird mysteriously disappeared. The tale so fascinated me that I began to seek out more information about this strange occurrence. I plunged deeply into the story and, in a way, made it my own. Not long afterwards, I was surprised to find myself telling it to friends. These were unmistakeable signs that I would soon be trapped inside some remote lighthouse myself, and that I'd end up like the protagonist of 'The Fog Horn', that exquisite Ray Bradbury story in which a sea monster answers the call of a tower's sound and light, and emerges from the deep, longing to embrace it.

THERE IS SOMETHING BEAUTIFUL and wild in these impossible architectures. Perhaps because we sense that these creatures are dying. Their lights are going out, their bodies crumbling. And although many of these sentries remain determined to fulfil their mission of illuminating the waters, nowadays new technologies of maritime communication make their function ever more superfluous. Ships no longer need to be under their romantic guardianship, and new guides have arrived – satellites in orbit, GPS navigation, sonar, radar – to make us forget that lighthouses have been the homes and workplaces of men and women, often anonymous ones. With the passing of time, the number of automated signals increases. Some abandon their original purpose to transform themselves into tourist destinations. Others, less fortunate, are discreetly dismantled. Most lighthouse-keepers, symbols of vigilance and protection, have left their duties behind. Yet although that life is about to fade away, we will still have their stories. The ruins in the form of words from a time when technology and heroism were one and the same thing. Because in lighthouses, and especially in isolated lighthouses, humans have always been at the mercy of nature.

And so this is not just a book about lighthouses. It is also a way of seeing ourselves reflected in the mirror of the human condition, of questioning ourselves about the experience of living in solitude, of recognizing other people's dependence upon the challenge of survival, of exploring the depths to which we can sink and the heights to which we can soar in extreme situations. The emptiness we feel when we are not sheltered by our fellow creatures can be a hell for some. For others, meanwhile, like Charles Bukowski, 'isolation is the gift'.

Jules Verne wrote his adventure novel *The Lighthouse at the End of the World* inspired by a small lighthouse that shone briefly in Patagonia at the end of the nineteenth century. He described the Isla de los Estados without ever having set foot on Argentine soil – just as he hadn't on the moon, or in the centre of the earth, or at the bottom of the sea – yet he constructed a magnificent tale. I have likewise been swimming around for almost two years in a sea of information, trying to distinguish the lights from the shadows in the hope of making some often hard-to-prove stories seem credible. Nothing is invented, and everything written in this book has been written previously somewhere else. Despite never having been to any of these isolated lighthouses, I have allowed myself to behave as though I knew them and I have felt – from my contemporary comfort – the storms lashing the windows, the isolation looming behind the tempests, the solitude lurking in the fog.

A HUGE MICHELIN WORLD MAP hangs from the wall. Every day, particularly in these strange times of not being able to travel, I allow my gaze to be lost on its surface and let myself be guided by chance. Reading a name written alongside a black dot or observing a space delimited by a line compels me to begin an imaginary journey, and swiftly I am transported there. Perhaps that is why I conceived of this project as an atlas. But unlike the infinite expanses I think I can see on my map, this book is short and limited. Choosing which dots are highlighted on the plan and which are not has been one of the more complicated questions. I am aware that many noteworthy and attractive lighthouses that could convey captivating stories have been omitted.

I hope that, through these stories, drawings and maritime charts, you will experience an epic journey to distant places and times, and enjoy as much as I have the confinement – sometimes comforting, sometimes sinister – that you will find presented in these pages.

JOSÉ LUIS GONZÁLEZ MACÍAS
SEPTEMBER 2020

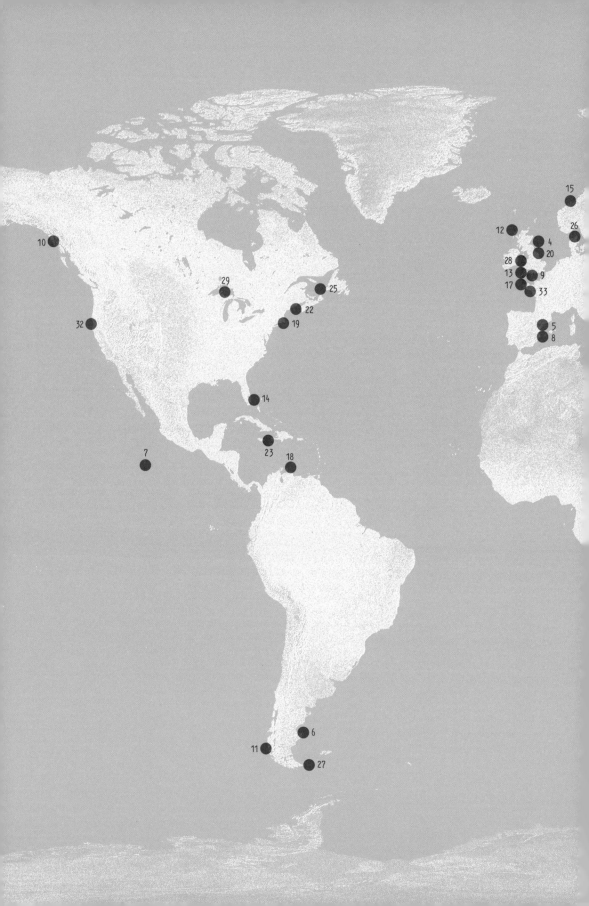

1   Adziogol Lighthouse

CLOSE TO RYBALCHE, the tarmacked road comes to an end. Beyond are the sands of Kinburn, a place far from civilization where golden dunes meet coastal salt marshes and coniferous forests. These steppe lands were once inhabited by the Amazons. According to Herodotus, none but Hercules could defeat them.

Further into the water, a kilometre and a half from Rybalche, where the Dnipro River meets the Black Sea, a slender structure has stood for over a hundred years. Its presence is still necessary. Piloting a boat to Kherson, up a Dnipro cloaked in the persistent autumn fog, entails a labyrinthine journey between small fluvial islands, convoluted river-branches and dredged waterways in a complex estuary.

IT IS LIKELY THAT, in exchange for a bit of money, some tins of beer and a few litres of petrol, a curious traveller would be able to persuade some local fisherman to get them close to the lighthouse. With a bit of luck, they might get inside the vast frame, a gleaming red metal web, and climb, as though mounting the wings of a giant insect, the narrow stairway. Hidden in the base of the tower is a small shelter for the lighthouse-keepers. Although they could reach the lighthouse daily from the coast, on a boat in the warmer seasons or by walking across the ice in the winter, the sudden changes of weather sometimes made their return impossible for weeks. Nothing here is superfluous.

THE RUSSIAN ENGINEER AND SCIENTIST Vladimir Shukhov sketched lines with all the precision of the Ukrainian women who stitched together the threads of their *hustkas*, or shawls. To look at his structures, drawn on paper, you might logically think that they would collapse if a light breeze happened to blow in the right direction. However, his sketches were as firm as they were fine. At the end of the nineteenth century, he imagined towers, roofs, pavilions and buildings able to support themselves with the least amount of materials possible. He managed to breathe life into simple steel-mesh frames, transforming them into pieces of architecture that were extraordinary, organic, light, not subject to the rules of time.

These hyperboloid drawings synthesized efficiency, simplicity and elegance and, after the 1917 revolution, imbued Soviet architecture with the constructivist spirit. Shukhov is considered one of history's outstanding Russian engineers.

THE ADZIOGOL LIGHTHOUSE was devised to resemble a wicker basket, with hundreds of holes, open for the wind to pass through.

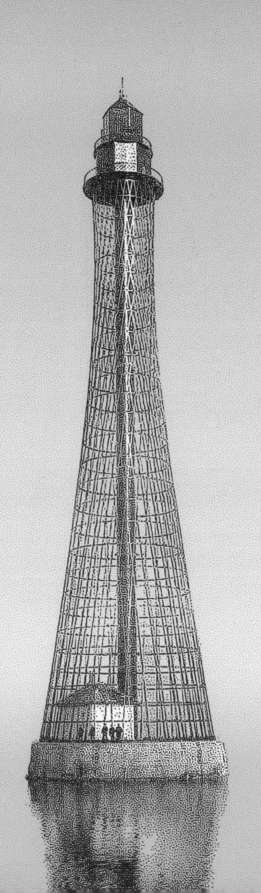

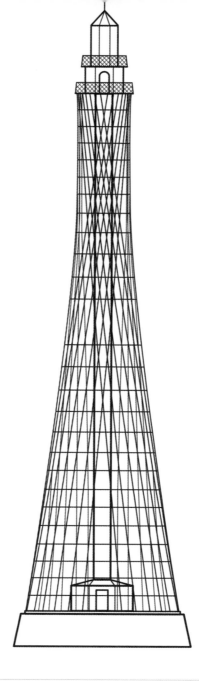

1

**Adziogol
Lighthouse**

BLACK SEA
EUROPE

46° 29′ 32″ N
32° 13′ 57″ E

Engineer: Vladimir Shukhov
Date of construction: 1908–11
Date of lighting: 1911
Active
Hyperboloid steel tower
Height of tower: 64m
Focal height: 67m
Range: 19 n.m.
Light characteristic: fixed white light

Adziogol has set several height records.
It is the tallest single-section structure
built by Shukhov. It is also the tallest
lighthouse in Ukraine, the nineteenth in
the world and the tallest in this book.

If you built an Eiffel Tower with a
hyperboloid structure similar to that of
the Adziogol Lighthouse, it would weigh
just a third of what it actually does.

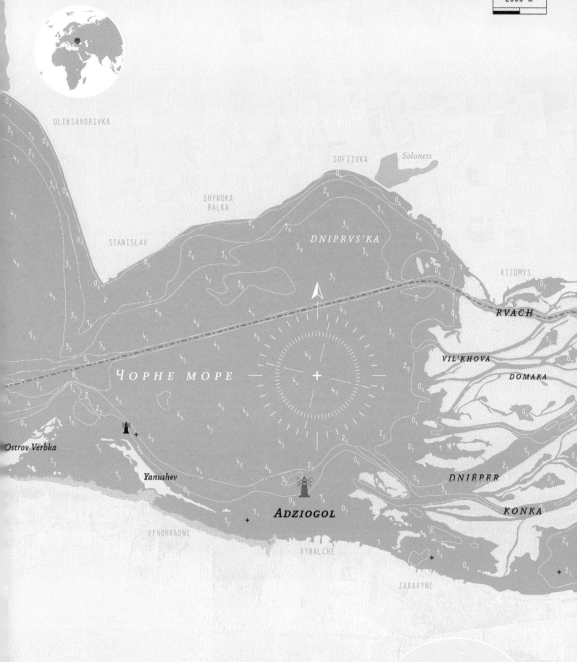

2000 m

OLEKSANDRIVKA

SOFIIVKA   Solonets

SHYROKA
BALKA

DNIPRVS'KA

STANISLAV

KIZOMYS

RVACH

VIL'KHOVA

DOMAKA

Чорне море

Ostrov Verbka

Yanushev

DNIÈPER

KONKA

ADZIOGOL

VYNOHRADNE

RYBALCHE

ZABARYNE

Rybal'chans'ke   Pyvnyv

UKRAYINA
Україна

Odzhyhol

CHORNE MORE
Чорне море

2

Amédée Lighthouse

AMÉDÉE,
NOUMÉA,
NEW
CALEDONIA
(FRANCE)

ON THE DANGEROUS ROCHES-DOUVRES REEF, almost 40 kilometres from the Brittany coast, a large cast-iron lighthouse was erected in 1867. This tower lit up the waters between two islands, Bréhat and Guernsey, until it was destroyed by German troops in 1944. Fortunately, the old Roches-Douvres lighthouse has a surviving twin in the antipodes.

THE FRENCH EMPIRE colonized New Caledonia in the mid-nineteenth century. On this island, previously explored on voyages by Cook and Lapérouse, it found the ideal territory for locating a prison – less notorious than the one in Guiana – to which it could transport dangerous convicts and political prisoners sentenced after the growing popular revolts in France. The legislators described this earthly paradise, formerly frequented by whalers, sandalwood dealers and unlicensed fishermen, as *one of the locations best suited to hosting our prisons.*

The entrance to the port of the recently founded city of Nouméa was protected by a huge reef. Sailing through the Boulari Pass, among hundreds of coral islets and constant changes in the swell, was not without difficulty, and wrecks like that of the *L'Aventure* in 1827 soon prompted the need to build a lighthouse. Although the small island of Amédée was chosen for its location, the tower was originally conceived more than 16,000 kilometres away, in the metropolis that styled itself *the city of light.*

In Paris, the Rigolet company built the mechanical structures that were later transported in pieces to the coast; and the workshops of the watchmaker Henry-Lepaute, in addition to turning mechanisms, also built those optics designed by Augustin Fresnel thanks to which seas across the world would be flooded with light.

The tower destined for New Caledonia first rose up majestically in the Villette neighbourhood in 1862, and that summer the residents of the capital had the opportunity to see its silhouette before the sailors did. Two years later, it was parcelled up into 1,200 boxes. The almost 400-tonne cargo travelled down the Seine on barges to the port of Le Havre and crossed the seas in the hold of the *Émile Pereire*. Progress in the form of light arrived at the new colony. On 15 November 1865, the Amédée lighthouse was inaugurated with religious rites, military pomp and showy speeches from the authorities.

THANKS TO THIS BEACON, the ships carrying political prisoners arrived safely in New Caledonia. Who can say whether some French citizen might have looked at this tower as it travelled through Paris and then, sometime later, espied its light from a Nouméa cell?

2

Amédée
Lighthouse

Coral Sea,
Pacific Ocean
Oceania

22° 28′ 38″ S
166° 28′ 05″ E

Date of construction: 1862
Date of lighting: 1865
Automated: 1985
Active
Conical tower of cast iron
Height of tower: 56m
Focal height: 59m
Range: 24.5 n.m.
Light characteristic: two white flashes
every 15 seconds

It is possible to send a letter from
Amédée. The tower contains a small
post office and has its own stamp
commemorating the lighthouse.

The spiral staircase that leads up to
the platform and the lamp has 247
wrought-iron steps.

Aniva Lighthouse

IN THE VAST DARKNESS of the seas of the USSR, ships navigated using the occasional distant lighthouses that illuminated their waters. The high cost of maintaining these stations, whose energy supply often proved unviable, forced the Soviet leaders to opt for a risky alternative to guarantee their continued operation. During the Cold War, the lamps of more than a hundred and thirty Russian lighthouses were fuelled by RTGs – radioisotope thermoelectric generators. These devices resembled miniature nuclear power stations and produced energy from the heat generated by the decay of radioactive material. RTGs have often been used in satellites, space probes and the remotest facilities – inaccessible places where it's not easy to change a battery.

THE LONG, NARROW ISLAND of Sakhalin, inhabited by people from Japan, Russia and China, had been disputed since the seventeenth century, but when the Second World War ended, its territory was annexed by the USSR. At the far south-west, in 1939, an unusual Japanese lighthouse was erected, originally called Nakashiretoko. A tower that, like a castle in a fairytale, was delicately placed by the engineer Shinobu Miura on the Sivuchya rock just off the sheer Cape Aniva. But the Japanese only took care of its lamp for a decade. After the signing of the Treaty of San Francisco, they were obliged to withdraw from the island. The lighthouse operated for another forty years, thanks to the toil of Russian workers, with the energy supplied by diesel engines, until in the 1990s – when the Soviet flag was lowered from the Kremlin – it was automated with a radioisotope nuclear generator. The lighthouse-keepers left the facilities from one day to the next and the logbook, forgotten on Aniva, fell silent for ever.

THE LIGHT HAS NOT BEEN IN OPERATION for more than a decade. Without its glare, thousands of seabirds have taken possession of the tower. The passage of time has left its traces on the desolate facilities: flaking walls, rust on the buildings, the old engines plundered and broken glass in the windows. Small boats with daring tourists arrive at its vicinity in search of abandoned places, an activity the Japanese call *haikyo*. If the sea allows, they take selfies at the feet of its ruins.

Although the authorities have given assurances that the radioisotope generator has been dismantled, one of its walls still bears the words, handwritten in large letters: *Danger, nuclear radiation!*

FOCAL PLANE OF LIGHT

SEA LEVEL

3

Aniva
Lighthouse

Sea of Okhotsk,

Pacific Ocean

Asia

46° 01′ 07″ N
143° 24′ 51″ E

Engineer: Shinobu Miura
Date of construction: 1937–39
Date of lighting: 1939
Automated: 1990
Deactivated: 2006
Cylindrical concrete tower
Height of tower: 31m
Focal height: 40m
Range: 15.2 n.m.

Fifty years before the lighthouse was built, Anton Chekhov travelled to Sakhalin Island. He described it as a *frozen hell*.

It is possible to reach the lighthouse by motorboat from the village of Novikovo, located around 40 kilometres away by sea.

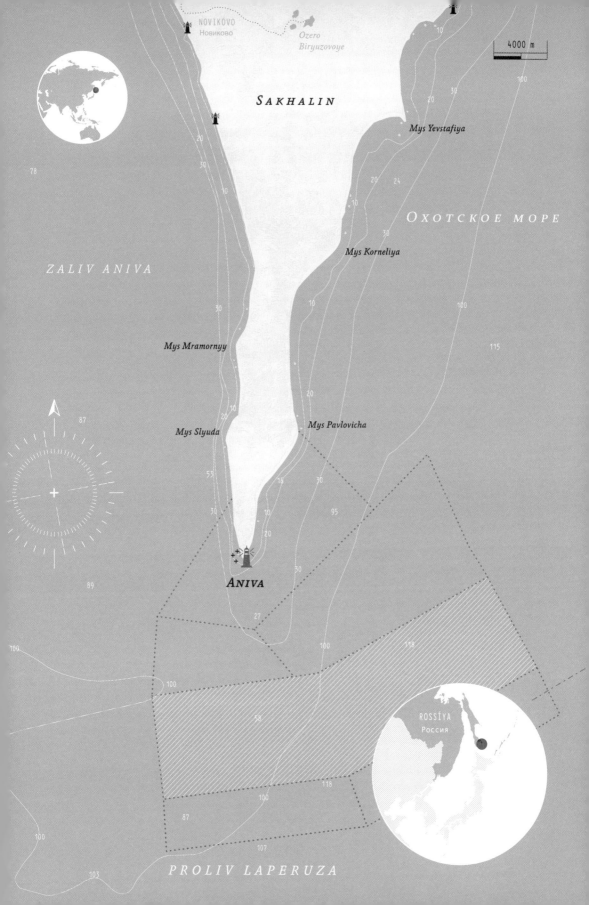

NOVIKOVO
Новиково

*Ozero
Biryuzovoye*

SAKHALIN

4000 m

Mys Yevstafiya

78

20

30

10

20

24

ОХОТСКОЕ МОРЕ

10

30

Mys Korneliya

ZALIV ANIVA

10

100

30

115

Mys Mramornyy

20

87

30
20

10

Mys Slyuda

Mys Pavlovicha

53

16

30

10

95

89

30

10

20

ANIVA

30

27

100

118

109

100

118

58

ROSSIYA
Россия

100

118

87

100

100

107

103

PROLIV LAPERUZA

4   Bell Rock Lighthouse

ACCORDING TO ONE LEGEND, the Abbot of Arbroath placed a bell activated by the waves on the Inchcape Rock to warn ships of the dangerous presence of a reef that was hidden, most of the time, under the waters. A pirate by the name of Ralph borrowed the bell for himself, then forgot about the robbery and was wrecked years later, in the same place.

AS THOUGH WALKING UPON THE WATERS of the North Sea, sixty men are striving to bore into a rock. They are up to their knees in water, 18 kilometres from the nearest coast, and they're working as fast as they can, because in just two hours the tide will cover them completely. Before that happens they return to the *Smeaton* and the *Pharos* at anchor nearby and spend the rest of the day in the swaying swell. By the time autumn comes, they have excavated a foundation 13 metres in diameter and constructed shelters that will allow them to stay there and to store materials during the next season of work. The following summer, they manage to lay the first stone. One by one, they would put down another 2,500 to raise the lighthouse. Each stone weighs a ton. Each has been shaped with care and secured with wooden pegs in such a way that, like a jigsaw, it will slot into the previous one. The works continue for another three years and fatal accidents occur, as well as the desertion of workers unable to bear the inclemencies of the sea and labour mutinies prompted by the shortage of beer. Finally, the light of Bell Rock is lit on 1 February 1811.

BELL ROCK IS THE OLDEST LIGHTHOUSE erected in the open sea that is still standing. Its strength is the result of a collective effort by people who are anonymous: labourers, sailors, foremen, stonemasons . . . though the success of the construction can be attributed to two men. Robert Stevenson, the grandfather of the famous author of *Treasure Island* – young, impetuous and perhaps a little arrogant – dreamed of erecting a lighthouse in a place that seemed impossible to conquer. He planned the project, persuaded the Northern Lighthouse Board of its viability and remained in charge of all the construction work, enduring its hardships and its risks. John Rennie, the chief engineer, hardly visited the rock. From his office in London, he confirmed the calculations and suggested technical solutions so that the frame might withstand the harshness of the Scottish sea.

    The lighthouse's design was related, albeit indirectly, to the encounter of a man and a tree. Bell Rock was modelled on plans that fifty years earlier had been built on the isolated Eddystone Reef on the south coast of England. John Smeaton, its engineer, had devised its structure after witnessing how an old oak remained upright, without bowing, in the middle of a powerful storm.

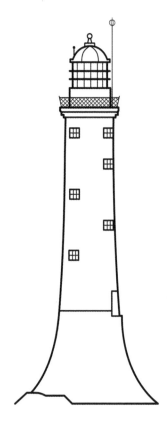

4

Bell Rock Lighthouse

North Sea,
Atlantic Ocean
Europe

56° 25′ 58″ N
02° 23′ 17″ W

Engineer: Robert Stevenson
Date of construction: 1807–10
Date of lighting: 1811
Automated: 1988
Active
Cylindrical Aberdeen granite tower
Height of tower: 35.3m
Focal height: 28m
Range: 18 n.m.
Light characteristic: one white flash at
15-second intervals

The author and BBC producer Deborah
Cadbury named Bell Rock one of the
Seven Wonders of the Industrial World,
alongside the Brooklyn Bridge, the
Hoover Dam and the Panama Canal.

In 1819, Stevenson commissioned
a picture of Bell Rock from Turner.
The famous artist – who, according to
legend, once had himself tied to a ship's
mast during a storm in order to paint
*Snow Storm: Steam-Boat off a Harbour's
Mouth* – produced a watercolour from
his studio, without ever visiting the site.

Deil's Heid

ARBROATH

EAST HAVEN

RNOUSTIE

NORTH SEA

2000 m

BELL ROCK

INT ANDREWS BAY

WORMISTON

UNITED
KINGDOM

5   Buda Lighthouse

THE ISLAND OF BUDA is a shifting island, which drifts slowly in the Mediterranean. It advances and retreats; it dwindles and grows with the passing of time. Buda is an island of silt, which sprouted out of the depths of the delta at the start of the eighteenth century from the patient accumulation of sediments at the mouth of the Ebro. By the end of the 1950s, it had come to occupy almost 1,500 hectares, and about forty families settled there to grow rice. Today the rice-fields still grow on the land, but the major festivals, mass in the chapel and the football team have all disappeared; scarcely any people are left.

BEFORE THE LIGHTS CAME, ships would frequently run aground on those shifting sands. Trapped in a greyish sludge, after long death throes, they would plunge to the bottom. In the nineteenth century, three metal lighthouses were placed on the unstable coast, attached to screw piles, to illuminate the Ebro delta. One in the north, at the Punta del Fangar, one in the south at the Punta de la Baña, and the brightest on the island of Buda.

JOHN HENDERSON PORTER'S FACTORY in Birmingham produced a metal lighthouse dreamed up by a man from Madrid, the architect Lucio del Valle. The tower, the tallest of its kind, travelled by ship from England and its 187 tons were raised up on the shores of the Mediterranean. In November 1864, a lighthouse-keeper climbed 365 steps to light the first wick of an olive-oil-fuelled Degrand lamp. Then for over a century, the Buda lighthouse-keepers climbed those same steps every eight hours to wind the turning mechanism that controlled the optic.

THE BUDA LIGHTHOUSE was positioned at the end of Cape Tortosa, despite the fact that, if the delta grew too quickly, the light would soon be far removed from the sea. The sediments continued their advance for twenty years. By then, the lighthouse was so far inland that the waves could not be seen from its base. But around 1940, the sea began ferociously to devour the delta. The dams, the hydro-electric plant and the irrigation channels took tonnes of alluvium from the mouth of the Ebro. Storms and floods obliged the shores to beat a retreat. The island dwindled and bit by bit the lighthouse made its way into the sea.

It survived the dynamite placed by the Republican army during the Spanish Civil War. It held out against years of rust and corrosion with its foundations submerged. But a storm carried it off once and for all on Christmas Day, 1961. Now there is another lighthouse that shines beyond Cape Tortosa. The old metal lighthouse lies about four kilometres from the coast and rests there, forgotten, illuminating a shifting seabed.

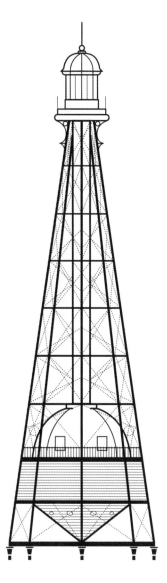

5

Buda Lighthouse

MEDITERRANEAN SEA
EUROPE

40° 43′ 07″ N
00° 54′ 55″ E

Engineer: Lucio del Valle
Date of construction: 1864
Date of lighting: 1864
Deactivated: 1961
Cylindrical wrought-iron tower
Height of tower: 50m
Focal height: 53m
Range: 20 n.m.

Madrid Polytechnic University houses a model of the Buda lighthouse, some two and a half metres tall. It was built in Barcelona and presented – along with models of other Spanish lighthouses, such as Finisterre, Corrubedo, Torre de Hércules, Cabo de Palos, Sisargas and Illa de l'Aire – at the Paris World's Fair in 1867.

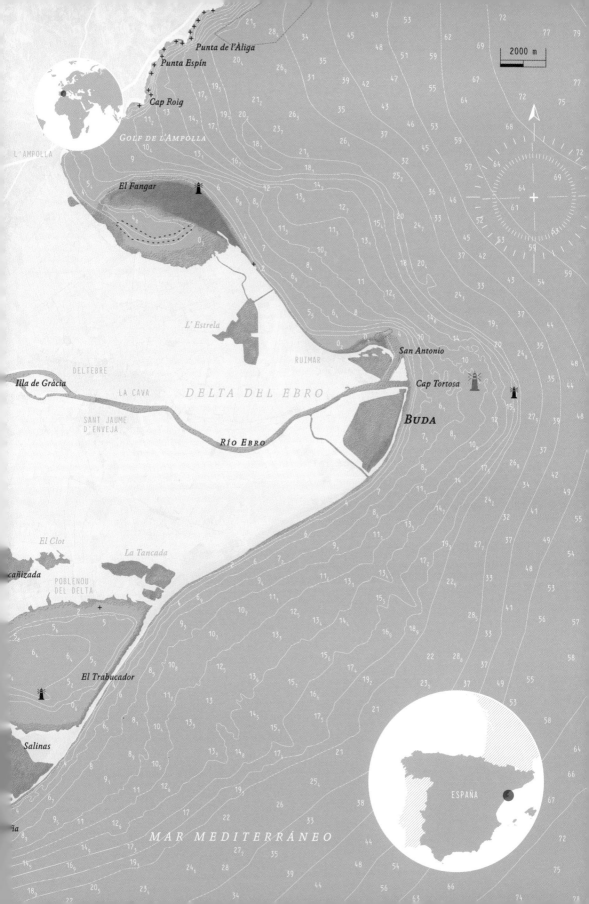

6 Cabo Blanco Lighthouse

Cabo Blanco,
Puerto
Deseado,
Santa Cruz
(Argentina)

Provincial Route 91, an unpredictable road covered in rubble and mud, peters out at the edge of a rocky crag. From there to Puerto Deseado – 90 kilometres of windswept plains – you will hardly meet another soul. The stone outcrop stretches from north to south, emerging at the coast like the scaly back of a dragon. The eyes of Ferdinand Magellan, Sir Francis Drake, Henry Cavendish and Charles Darwin all peered at its threatening silhouette from the ocean without ever daring to touch land. At the foot of the rock, on its seaward face, rests a small cemetery. Eight nameless crosses and a figure of the Virgin keep the silence of whoever lies beneath this arid ground.

The crag is crowned by a lighthouse. A hundred and fifteen steps climb from the path up to the base of the tower, and there are still another ninety-five beyond that before you can touch the light. From the lamp's balcony, if there were a 500-kilometre view, looking south-east out over the waters, you would see the Falklands. Much closer, if its lighthouse hadn't been abandoned over a century ago, you'd be able to make out the flashes from Penguin Island. But if your eyes could look back in time, facing away from the sea, in addition to the cemetery you could watch the activity of a salt mine, a telegraph office, a magistrate's court and a rugby pitch. At night, the lighthouse drags their ruins out of the darkness just the same way as it illuminates the seals resting on the beach. This light fades away towards the interior that is either the beginning or the end – no one knows – of Patagonia. This is the loneliest and least hospitable of Argentina's lighthouses.

By torchlight, a ghost story is told. In the 1950s, one of the lighthouse-keepers, a naval ensign, was known for his habit of writing on a typewriter. One grim day, he was found slumped over it, suffering from terrible pains. His companion raced off for help, but by the time he returned, the sick man had already died. Since then, the night-time silence is broken by the sound of typewriter keys being struck, a typed message of warning for whoever cannot bear the solitude.

There was a time when the old lighthouse was set to be abandoned, but the light remains active and the men run it diligently. The keepers' house has views of the sea. It's large, so spacious that it can fit almost everything: a gas heater, a ping-pong table, a chessboard and an old Remington typewriter still loaded with its black ink ribbon.

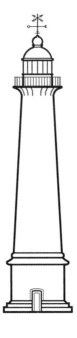

6

Cabo Blanco
Lighthouse

Atlantic Ocean

South America

47° 12′ 01″ S
65° 44′ 03″ W

Date of construction: 1915–17
Date of lighting: 1917
Active
Truncated cone-shaped brick tower
Height of tower: 26.7m
Focal height: 67m
Range: 13.9 n.m.
Light characteristic: one white flash at
10-second intervals

There is a reference to Cabo Blanco
in Jules Verne's *Journey to the Centre
of the Earth*. In 1864, the year of its
publication, the lighthouse did not yet
exist.

110,000 trapezoidal bricks were used
to raise the tower. They came from the
same factory as those in the Buenos
Aires metro and La Plata Cathedral.

Another Cabo Blanco lighthouse,
on the island of Mallorca, marks the
western limits of the Bay of Palma.

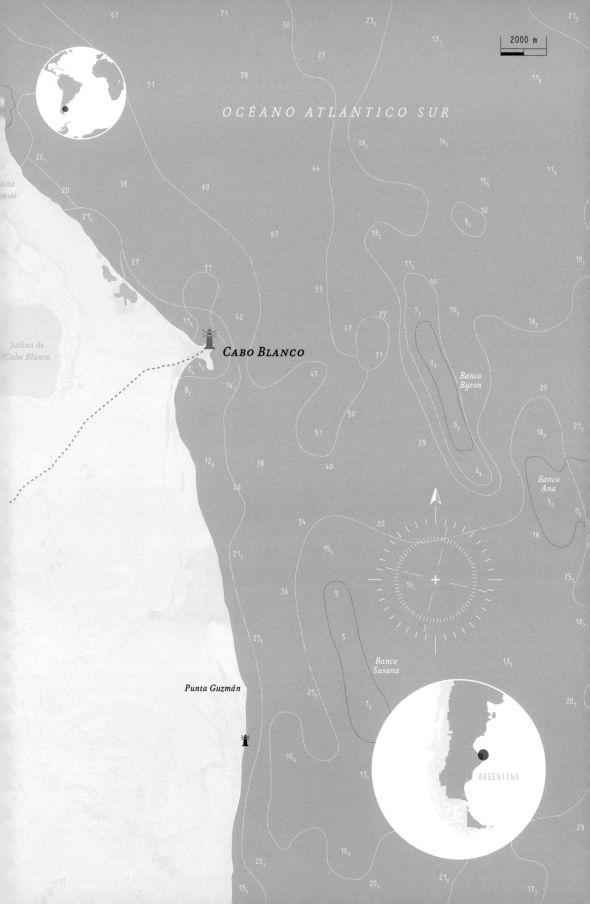

OCÉANO ATLÁNTICO SUR

CABO BLANCO

Salina de
Cabo Blanco

Banco
Byron

Banco
Ana

Banco
Susana

Punta Guzmán

ARGENTINA

2000 m

Clipperton Lighthouse

As tropical paradises go, Clipperton – which the French call the Île de la Passion – enjoys little popularity. Lost in the vastness of the Pacific, it stinks of ammonia, it gets lashed by hurricanes, its beaches are invaded by crabs and its waters infested with sharks. The small lighthouse here has been irrelevant in the history of maritime navigational signalling, but the incidents it has witnessed have not been carried away with the wind. By way of confirmation, a photo has been preserved, taken in 1917 on the deck of a warship, showing four women and seven children – its final inhabitants.

Around 1906, a small Mexican military detachment and their families settle here to claim sovereignty. In command is Ramón Arnaud, a young sergeant who boasts of being the governor of this remote place. When the revolution breaks out in Mexico, the only ship that supplies them is set alight by the insurgents and the expected provisions end up at the bottom of the sea off the Mazatlán coast. With no news of what has happened and abandoned to their luck, the islanders suffer malnutrition and scurvy. For over a year, life on Clipperton occurs in total isolation, until in 1915, a US schooner accidentally runs aground on its reefs. When the US Navy sends a boat to rescue its compatriots, it offers the craft for evacuating the twenty-seven surviving islanders, too. But Arnaud refuses. He does not allow any of the Mexicans to leave the island. What awaits most of them is death or insanity.

One September morning, Arnaud, possibly delirious, sights a ship on the horizon and yells out to the local garrison: *Cardona! Guerra! Rodríguez!* Accompanied by his men, he rushes out to sea in a small boat. The others watch powerlessly from the beach as, in the distance, the boat sinks.

Only women and children remain on the island, and one solitary, elusive man, the lighthouse-keeper Victoriano Álvarez. Overtaken by madness, he entrenches himself in the lighthouse with a firearm and proclaims himself King of Clipperton. He establishes a reign of terror, enslaving the women and forcing them to fulfil his sexual desires. When one of them refuses, he kills her. His 'reign' lasts almost two years, until Alicia Rovira, Arnaud's widow, and the young Tirza Randon manage, with hammer-blows and stabs, to put an end to the lighthouse-keeper's life. Moments later, they spot a ship on the horizon. The gunboat USS *Yorktown* is headed towards the island.

Clipperton would be left deserted for ever after. At the foot of its lighthouse lies a disfigured body, covered in crabs.

7

**Clipperton
Lighthouse**

PACIFIC OCEAN

AMERICA

10° 18′ 14″ N
109° 13′ 04″ W

Engineer: Eugène de Michelon
Date of construction: 1906
Date of lighting: 1906
Deactivated: between 1917 and 1935,
and from 1938
Cylindrical concrete tower
Height of tower: 6m
Focal height: 12m

In the nineteenth century, Mexico
and France had a dispute over the
sovereignty of Clipperton which lasted
twenty-two years, until the arbitration
of Victor Manuel III – the King of Italy –
found in favour of the French. Although
it was they who built the lighthouse,
they never actually got to settle on the
island permanently.

In 1978, Jacques Cousteau shot
Clipperton: The Island Time Forgot,
a documentary in which Ramón
Arnaud Rovira, who survived the 1917
evacuation, returns to his birthplace.

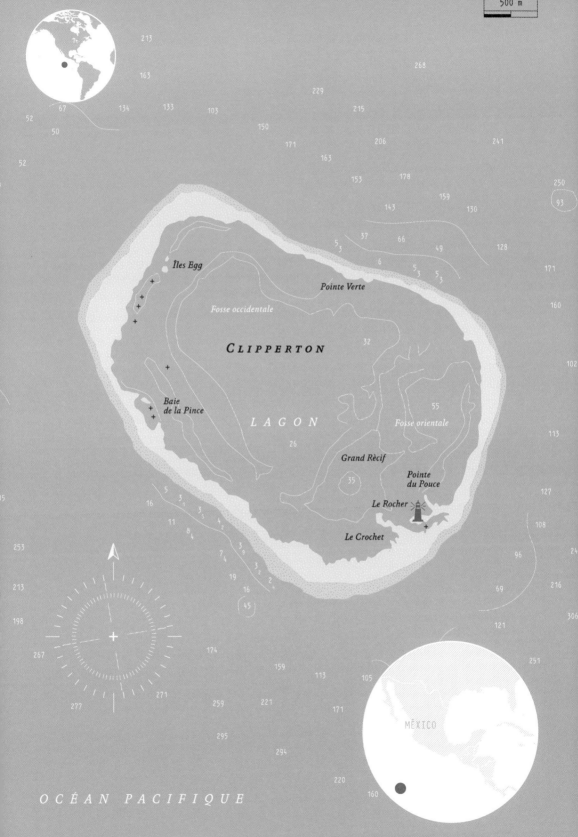

500 m

213

163

268

229

215

67   134   133   103

52

50   150

52   171   206   241

9   163

153   178   250

143   159   130   93

37   66   49   128

5   6   171

Îles Egg   Pointe Verte   5   5   3

3   3

160

Fosse occidentale   32

CLIPPERTON   102

55

Baie
de la Pince   L A G O N   Fosse orientale   113

26   Grand Rècif

Pointe
du Pouce   127

35

Le Rocher   108

5   3   Le Crochet   24

16   3   5   96   216

11   4   2

8   4   69   121

7   4   306

19   3   253

16   2   4   251

45   174   159

213   113   105

198   171   MÉXICO

267   271   221

277   259

295

294

220   OCÉAN   PACIFIQUE   160

8

Columbretes Lighthouse

Opposite the coast of Castellón, some 50 kilometres to the east, the remains of a crater surface as rocks that twist reptile-like on the waters of the Mediterranean. They are the so-called islands of snakes, *columbraria*; stunning, wild, solitary.

Before the arrival of the lighthouse, nobody lived here. The rocks served only as a passing refuge for fishermen, smugglers and pirates. Apart from the isolation and the storms, the place hid another type of danger: the land was overrun by scorpions and snakes. Building the lighthouse required clearing the terrain, a task assigned to prisoners condemned to capital punishment who were promised the remittance of their sentences. Many of those who were first there didn't survive the stings, while the rest dug ditches and filled them with lime to keep themselves apart from such dangerous company.

In 1859, a light came on over the Illa Grossa, the largest of the islands, and the lighthouse-keepers arrived with their families to watch over its blaze. Conditions were harsh to begin with, shifts lasted an entire year of solitude and the only people who ended up there were those who had no other option. Some couldn't bear it; a Majorcan towerman took his own life on learning that Columbretes would be his next posting.

But most of the keepers went on with their day-to-day lives and, as time passed, life on the island became easier. The vipers were eradicated with fires, with pigs and chickens. Scorpions were avoided using cans filled with water placed at the legs of beds. Two or three families shared their lives around the lighthouse and there were many things to do on Columbretes: tend to the lamp, repair the vaporizers, clean the lenses, refill the kerosene, fix the damage from the autumn storms, wind the mechanism, grow potatoes in the kitchen garden, fish for lobsters, knead the bread, hunt rabbits, watch the army planes doing their target practice, feed the chickens, monitor the level of the cistern, run along the cliffs, catch scorpions with a piece of cotton thread, visit the cemetery that was the eternal resting-place of some lighthouse-keepers and just a few shipwrecks, teach the children their lessons, protect themselves when the storms arrived, marvel at the island covered in white flowers after a few days of rain and wait for provisions every week and a half or two.

According to the Austrian archduke Ludwig Salvator, who lived with the lighthouse-keepers, studied the islands, and in 1895 published an extensive, meticulous book about them, *the life of the inhabitants of Columbretes is happy as that of the quail, the lark, the thrush and the turtledove, which come in spring and autumn to rest here and then fly on to the neighbouring continent, or further, towards the north.*

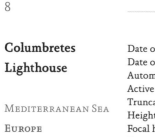

8

Columbretes Lighthouse

39° 53′ 44″ N

00° 41′ 06″ E

Date of construction: 1855–59
Date of lighting: 1859
Automated: 1986
Active
Truncated cone-shaped masonry tower
Height of tower: 20m
Focal height: 85m
Range: 21 n.m.
Light characteristic: a pair of flashes followed by one flash of white light every 22 seconds

Las Columbretes is a protected area. The 19 hectares above the surface make up a Nature Reserve. The 5,500 hectares of surrounding waters are a Marine Reserve.

Aïllats, the memory of Columbretes is a magnificent documentary directed by Patricia González, Eva Mestre, Xavi del Señor and Fernando Ramia, which recounts the lives of the islands' inhabitants.

52

61

63

54

65

82

52

59

64

78

84

52

56

68

88

85

58

51

53

58

68

55

82

47 45 11

52

51

79

62

38

85

60

54

39

82

61

63

60

COLUMBRETE GRANDE O ILLA GROSSA

81

57

51

Puerto Tofiño

38

COLUMBRETES

57

54

El Mancolibre

83

59

44

17

82

60

57

51

25

El Mascarat

70

57

41

57

43 25

61

80

Malaspina 38 **Bauza**

65

82

84

26

66

68

70

Navarrete 43 54

46

65

75

27 22

26

73

77

78

39 34

32

45

70

54

48

65

69

52

73

77

80

51

67

40 46

72

55

53

24 **Banco Jorge Juan**

73

67

78

62

56

Joaquín

71

76

46

39

69

73

54

38

16

59

78

La Horada **Lobo** 60

72

61

Méndez Núñez

69

71

37

73

76

64

65

45

41

37

72

66

41

46

60

48

57

74

44

56

74

67

48

74

52

42

68

74

64

48

57

79

55

18

30

76

56

20

79

16

80

67

El Bergantín

46

Churruca

76

Cerquero

10

80

Baleato **Banco de Luyando**

66

53

Banco de Patiño

30

16

12

75

30

44

64

ESPAÑA

Eddystone Lighthouse

IN ONE OF the National Museum of Scotland's collections, you can see a dark object, flat and oval-shaped, weighing about 200 grams. The accompanying text reads: *A piece of lead taken from the stomach of a keeper after the fire of 1755.*

It is the night of 2 December, and the lamp in the Rudyard Tower, off the Plymouth coast, is ablaze. Keeper Henry Hall, aged ninety-four and still active, tries to stifle the fire by throwing buckets of water towards the upper level. Because of the flames, the lead roof melts and a piece of molten metal falls into his mouth. Despite this, Henry Hall keeps struggling alongside his companions to get the fire under control. On the verge of exhaustion, the fire still raging, the lighthouse-keepers take refuge on a nearby crag until, eight hours later, a boat transports them to the shore.

Henry Hall survives another twelve days. The physician Edward Spry, who carries out the post-mortem, writes a report for the Royal Society giving an account of events, to the disbelief of some. Dr Spry spends the rest of his days obsessed with restoring his reputation and carries out repeated experiments on dogs and birds, pouring molten lead into their throats, to demonstrate that they could remain alive.

THE RUDYARD TOWER was destroyed. But it wasn't the first lighthouse to occupy Eddystone Rock, nor would it be the last. Fifty-seven years earlier, the Winstanley Tower had been built in this same exposed location, becoming the first lighthouse in the world located in the open seas.

HENRY WINSTANLEY was an eccentric businessman who loved architecture, hydraulic machinery and automated contraptions. After several of his ships were wrecked on the reef, he erected a delicate lighthouse that looked better suited to decorating a dolls' house than withstanding the inclemencies of the sea. While he was assembling this precious Meccano set in the waters of the English Channel, a French ship seized him and carried him off to France as a prisoner. When King Louis XIV learned of the incident, he ordered his immediate release, saying: *France is at war with England, not with humanity.*

Winstanley returned to Eddystone, and though his first lighthouse was destroyed by a storm, he managed to erect an even more beautiful second tower that remained upright until 1703. He believed absolutely in the solidity of this latest construction, even stating that he would want to be inside it during *the greatest storm there ever was.* Ill luck or rashness meant that on 26 November, Winstanley was indeed on Eddystone. That night, a violent cyclone known as the Great Storm devastated the English coast, dragging the tower and all its occupants to the bottom of the sea.

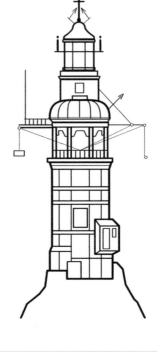

9

Eddystone Lighthouse

ENGLISH CHANNEL,
ATLANTIC OCEAN

EUROPE

50° 10′ 48″ N
04° 15′ 54″ W

Winstanley Tower I

Engineer: Henry Winstanley
Date of construction: 1696
Date of lighting: 1698
Deactivated: 1699
Height of tower: 18m
Octagonal wooden tower

The first lighthouse erected in the open seas was built on the rocky Eddystone reef 14 kilometres from terra firma and about 19 from the port of Plymouth.

Winstanley Tower II

Engineer: Henry Winstanley
Date of construction: 1699
Date of lighting: 1699
Deactivated: 1703
Height of tower: 25m
Dodecagonal wooden tower

While the lighthouse was active, no shipwrecks were recorded. Two days after its disappearance in the Great Storm of 1703, the *Winchelsea* foundered on the reef and sank with a cargo of tobacco.

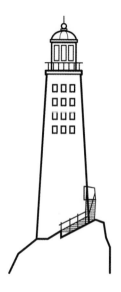

Rudyard Tower

Engineer: John Rudyard
Date of construction: 1708
Date of lighting: 1708
Deactivated: 1755
Height of tower: 21m
Conical tower of wood, brick and concrete

Captain John Lovett commissioned
Rudyard to build the lighthouse and, as
lessee, he charged the ships that were
aided by the light a toll of one penny per
ton.

Smeaton Tower

Engineer: John Smeaton
Date of construction: 1756
Date of lighting: 1759
Deactivated: 1877
Height of tower: 22m
Cylindrical conical granite tower

This tower marked a great advance in the
design of lighthouse structures. It was
dismantled and reconstructed in Plymouth
and today is a well-known monument in
its engineer's honour.

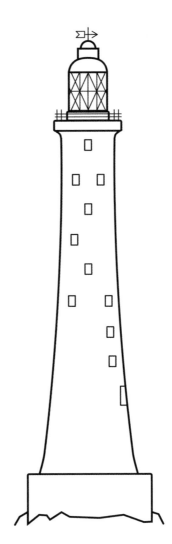

9

Eddystone Lighthouse

ENGLISH CHANNEL,
ATLANTIC OCEAN

EUROPE

50° 10′ 48″ N
04° 15′ 54″ W

Douglass Tower

Engineer: James Douglass
Date of construction: 1879
Date of lighting: 1882
Automated: 1982
Active
Cylindrical conical granite tower
Height of tower: 49m
Focal height: 41m
Range: 22 n.m.
Light characteristic: a pair of flashes
every 10 seconds

The Douglass Tower, the current
Eddystone Lighthouse, remains active
and stands beside the base of the now
dismantled Smeaton Tower.

In 1980, a helipad was built atop the
lamp to allow access for maintenance
personnel. Since 1999, the lighthouse
has been powered by solar energy.

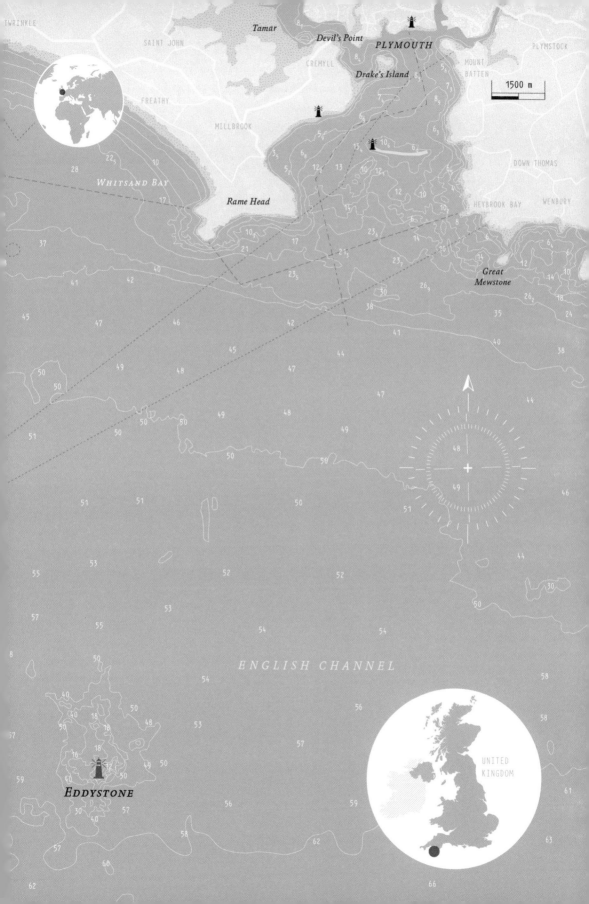

10   Eldred Rock Lighthouse

ELDRED ROCK,
LYNN CANAL,
HAINES,
ALASKA
(USA)

IN 1898, IN THE MIDDLE OF the Alaska gold rush, the *Clara Nevada* steamer travels through a storm down the Lynn Canal. It is transporting passengers, plus 800 pounds of precious metal and an illegal cargo hidden in the hold. Just 30 miles from its destination, it strikes a rock and suddenly catches fire. The consignment of dynamite it is carrying undercover has burst into flames.

According to the official report, there were no survivors, but a lifeboat was found nearby, and it's suspected that the captain and a few members of the crew did in fact survive the wreck. Despite the countless searches of the area carried out a century later, not a single gold nugget has been found among the ship's wreckage.

Accident or act of sabotage, what is certain is that the US Congress considered the event a compelling reason to build a lighthouse on Eldred Rock, the cold islet that was the *Clara Nevada*'s grave.

TEN YEARS LATER, during another violent tempest, a ghostly ship appears beached at the far northern end of Eldred Rock. For a few moments, the lighthouse illuminates the hull of the *Clara Nevada*. Its remains, like the living dead, have emerged just momentarily because of the storm.

THE KEEPER OF THE LIGHTHOUSE, Nils Peter Adamson, wakes from the middle of a nightmare, wanders over to the window and calls out the name of one of his assistants. The freezing early morning returns his voice to him in an echo, and then, silence.

Some days earlier, on 26 February 1910, John 'Scottie' Currie and John Silander, both assistants at Eldred Rock, travel three kilometres to the Point Sherwood Lighthouse for provisions. At dawn, accompanied by a light snowfall, they set off back to the lighthouse where Adamson is waiting for them. When he notices that his men are taking too long, he has a foreboding of some misfortune and calls for help. Boats comb the area, and even though the craft is located two days later, they find no trace of the men. Adamson, tormented by the possibility that his assistants might have drowned, trawls the cold waters of the Lynn Canal on his own for a month. *I myself am unable to account for any accident that could have happened to them, as there was no wind to speak of and a smooth sea & in my opinion they should have reached home easily by 8 p.m.* A year later, unable to bear the responsibility, he hands in his resignation as keeper of the lighthouse.

10

Eldred Rock
Lighthouse

Lynn Canal

Pacific Ocean

North America

58° 58′ 15″ N

135° 13′ 13″ W

Date of construction: 1905
Date of lighting: 1906
Automated: 1973
Active
Octagonal wooden tower
Height of tower: 17m
Focal height: 28m
Range: 8 n.m.
Original lens: Fresnel, 4th order
Light characteristic: one white flash at
6-second intervals

It was the naturalist Marcus Baker
who christened the islet, giving it the
maiden name of his wife, Sarah Eldred.

Though it is rather deteriorated,
this is the only lighthouse in Alaska
to retain its original structure. In
an attempt to maintain and restore
it, the Eldred Rock Lighthouse
Preservation Association was created,
in collaboration with the Sheldon
Museum.

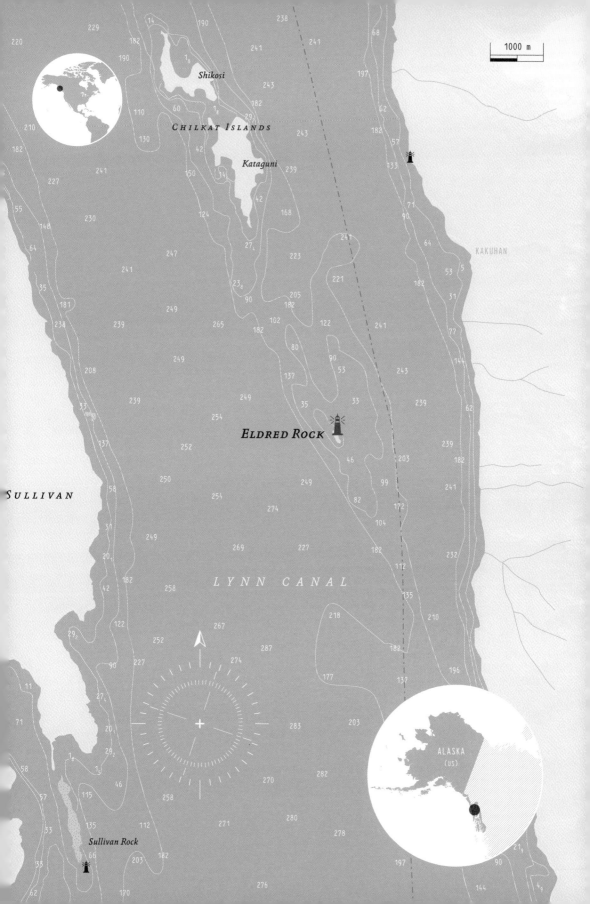

1000 m

Shikosi

CHILKAT ISLANDS

Kataguni

KAKUHAN

ELDRED ROCK

SULLIVAN

LYNN CANAL

ALASKA
(US)

Sullivan Rock

11   Evangelistas Lighthouse

EVANGELISTAS
ISLETS,
NATALES,
ÚLTIMA
ESPERANZA
(CHILE)

IN 1892, the Scottish engineer George Slight travelled from Edinburgh to the opposite end of the globe, his mind occupied by a complex challenge. On commission from the Chilean government, he was to erect a lighthouse at the western mouth of the Strait of Magellan. Sailing up the Pacific coast, he found himself before the craggy islets chosen for its location. He wrote in his diary:

I never imagined seeing something so wild and desolate as those emerging dark rocks in the middle of the raging waves. To see these stormy craggy rocks was frightening. With a dim light on the horizon we could see large waves crashing heavily in the western part of the islands: a vision that hardly anyone can imagine.

Slight would never leave Chile; he would oversee the construction of more than seventy lighthouses in that country. The first lamp to be lit was the Evangelistas Lighthouse, three years after that fearsome sight.

SPRING 1913. Long weeks of waiting go by, slowly. *La Yelcho*, a cutter of the Chilean Navy, is safely at anchor somewhere not far from Evangelistas. The ship is waiting for the weather to improve before it can supply the lighthouse with provisions and practical supplies. After more than forty days' delay, the sailors manage to reach the islet. On Evangelistas, after four months cut off, there is barely any food left and the lighthouse-keepers have had to resort to gathering kelp to feed themselves. When *La Yelcho* returns, it is carrying the body of Alfredo Sillard, the keeper who has died from an illness exacerbated by the tough conditions of isolation. The ship returns to the nearby cove they would thereafter call Forty Days, a solitary and inhospitable spot, to bury the lighthouseman's body. In time, this improvised cemetery is transformed into a place of worship. In the years that follow, whenever *La Yelcho* is forced to remain at anchor to await the meteorological conditions to allow it to reach the lighthouse, the sailors place candles on the lighthouseman's grave in the hope that his spirit might intercede against the storm.

Some keepers insist that they have felt the presence of Sillard's ghost wandering the lighthouse's rooms.

CHILEAN WRITERS like Rolando Cárdenas have been inspired by this story. Cárdenas's poem 'The Evangelistas Lighthouse Ghost' begins thus: *Far from the signals of the coast / supported on the planet's remotest depths / like four shadows rising from the sea. / Nothing but time beyond the archipelagos. / Time turned into a horizon, desperately empty, / into a persistent wind that would cling thunderously / to a thick water torn ceaselessly apart.*

The Evangelistas Lighthouse, with or without Sillard's ghost, is still inhabited today.

11

Evangelistas Lighthouse

Pacific Ocean

South America

52° 23′ 10″ S
75° 05′ 45″ W

Engineer: George Slight
Date of construction: 1895
Date of lighting: 1896
Active
Height of tower: 13m
Focal height: 58m
Range: 30 n.m.
Light characteristic: one white flash at
10-second intervals

On 28 November 1520, three ships under the command of Ferdinand Magellan sighted some craggy islets as they entered a huge ocean. It was the first time Europeans had sailed into the South Pacific. On a map produced in 1618 by the explorer García Nodal, these islets appear as *Los Evangelistas*.

In August 2019, Daniela Ortiz, a Chilean navy corporal in charge of telecommunications, became the first woman to be assigned the post of Evangelistas' lighthouse-keeper.

PACHECO

VICTORIA

OCÉANO PACÍFICO

ARCHIPIÉLAGO
REINA ADELAIDA

CUARENTA DÍAS

Elcano

Lobos

Evangelista

EVANGELISTAS

Pan de Azúcar

Roca Tortuga

Roca Ballenato

ESTRECHO DE
MAGALLANES

CHILE

2000 m

Flannan Isles Lighthouse

EILEAN MÒR,

FLANNAN ISLES,

OUTER HEBRIDES,

SCOTLAND

(UK)

THE FLANNAN ISLES – or Seven Hunters – form an uninhabited archipelago, 30 kilometres from the Outer Hebrides. On Eilean Mòr, the largest of these islands, there is a small chapel dedicated to St Flannan, a seventh-century abbot who was carried to these hostile lands by the accident of the winds. The place is laden with legends, and local sailors are known to employ unusual behaviours such as removing their hats when disembarking on the island or making a sunwise turn when they reach the peak. A solitary lighthouse was erected here in 1889.

ON 15 DECEMBER 1900, the first clue that there was something strange going on at the lighthouse was noticed by the steamer *Archtor* en route to Leith. The Flannan Isles lamp was unlit despite the adverse weather conditions. Eleven days later, on 26 December, the *Hesperus* managed to reach Eilean Mòr. It was being awaited on the island by lighthouse-keepers James Ducat, Thomas Marshall and Donald McArthur; the ship was bringing them supplies and a replacement keeper. But when the *Hesperus* approached the landing place, the crew saw that the flag was not flying on the platform, the boxes for provision were not in their usual position and nobody came out to meet them. From the ship, Captain Harvey sent up a flare and sounded the horn. No reply. Joseph Moore, the relief keeper, stepped onto the island. Through the thick fog, he climbed the slope until he reached the lighthouse. The main door was locked. He forced it open and gained access to the inside where he found the beds unmade, food on the plates and an upturned chair on the floor. A clock on the wall had stopped, showing 9:30. There was no trace of the men.

The sailors of the *Hesperus* combed every corner of the island trying to locate the keepers but they found only a number of unnerving clues. The lamps were clean and full of fuel. Only McArthur's overcoat was hanging from its hook. The other landing place, the one on the western side, seemed to have been damaged by a recent storm; there was a broken box tied to a derrick, the iron railings were bent out of shape and a heavy rock had collapsed onto the pier. In spite of this, the final entry in the log, written at 9 a.m. on 15 December, suggested that everything was in order.

THIRTY YEARS LATER, *Strange True Stories* magazine claimed that Marshall had written the following in his diary: *Dec. 12th Gale, north by north-west. Sea lashed to fury. [...] Never seen such a storm. Ducat irritable. [...] Storm still raging. Wind steady. Stormbound. Cannot go out. [...] Ducat quiet. McArthur crying. Dec 13th Storm continued through night. Wind shifted west by north. Ducat quiet. McArthur praying. 12 noon. Grey daylight. Me, Ducat and McArthur prayed. Dec 15th 1 p.m. storm ended. Sea calm. God is over all.*

12

Flannan Isles Lighthouse

ATLANTIC OCEAN

EUROPE

58° 17′ 18″ N
07° 35′ 16″ W

Engineer: Alan Stevenson
Date of construction: 1895–99
Date of lighting: 1899
Automated: 1971
Active
Cylindrical masonry tower
Height of tower: 23m
Focal height: 101m
Range: 20 n.m.
Current lens: Fresnel, 3rd order
Light characteristic: two white flashes every 30 seconds

The mysterious disappearance of the Flannan Isles lighthouse-keepers has led to much speculation, some of it paranormal, and inspired a whole host of fictional tales in literature, music and movies. The rock group Genesis tell the story in their song 'The Mystery of the Flannan Isle Lighthouse', and a 2018 psychological suspense movie directed by Kristoffer Nyholm takes the events as the main axis of its plot, though it was shot at four Scottish lighthouses, none of them the one on Eilean Mòr.

ATLANTIC OCEAN

39

64

50

61

42   43

44   41   10₅   37

33   5₂

52   37   22   26

37   34   26₃

37   28₅   27   30

24₅   27₃   31

95   42

35   31 16₅

40   20₅   32   37   26

Roaiream   20₅

Eilean
a'Ghobha   10₅

26₅

òna   40₅
'eit   41

24₅   35

FLANNAN ISLES
(*SEVEN HUNTERS*)

45

44

34   44

EILEAN MÒR

38   21

+

5₅

6   27

28

21
30

7₅

Eilean Tighe

26₅

37   31

33

37

10₅

27₅   31

Gealtir-Beg

38   35

33

26

27₅

30

34

33

31

22   42
42

42   37

43   35

39

43   37

37   42

39   39

42   39

43   43   35

36

45   37

40

40

36

46   36

40

40

42

23₅

34

34

35   34

22
22₅   11

+ +
+ +

22
22₅

36

38

10₅

14

32

19₉

15   31

+

33

21₅   32

25   36

24   34

39

938

31

35

40

36

39   37   498

35   40

42

Soraigh

37

40

498

13   Godrevy Lighthouse

VIRGINIA WOOLF WRITES the pages of *To the Lighthouse* – a work in which hardly anything happens, and in which a family is constantly postponing a trip to a lighthouse – as if the words are gushing out with a fluidity uncommon for her. Considered by *Time* magazine one of the greatest English-language novels of the twentieth century, it is inspired by the author's own experiences. As a girl, Virginia used to spend summers with her family in a house on the Cornish coast. On their walks, she could see the Godrevy Lighthouse from the shore, perched on the small craggy island in St Ives Bay. Those days would remain engraved in her memory many years later and, in some way, they would influence her novel, even if she located its plot a great distance away.

'It will rain,' he remembered his father saying. 'You won't be able to go to the Lighthouse.'

The Lighthouse was then a silvery, misty-looking tower with a yellow eye, that opened suddenly, and softly in the evening.

THE ENDLESS DEFERRALS to reaching the lighthouse did not happen only in the fiction of the novel. Many were the lighthouse-keepers who suffered from the delays to shipments or relief. At the end of 1925, while Virginia Woolf was feverishly writing her book in London, Godrevy's assistant keeper W. J. Lewis was completely alone: his companion had been evacuated to the land with pneumonia.

For eight long days, isolated on Godrevy, Lewis kept the light and the fog bell working uninterruptedly, waiting for a persistent storm to abate and a boat to arrive bringing a lighthouse-keeper to replace his companion. Where Woolf develops a novel with little dialogue, Lewis writes in his diary of his need to speak to somebody: *It was after fifty-four hours' constant watch keeping that I had to succumb to a few hours' sleep and felt so much refreshed that the coming night was not so much dreaded, even though I was beginning to feel the effects of loneliness. I craved for someone to talk with, and can hardly credit that for a week I never uttered a word either in speech or song, not even to myself.*

BOTH WOOLF AND LEWIS, isolated in their respective lighthouses, suffered the ravages of loneliness and wrote to exorcise their demons. In 1970, Lewis published a book entitled *Ceaseless Vigil*, into which he poured some of his distressing experiences. Virginia Woolf found no light to guide her to overcome the pain caused in part by her inability to communicate. In March 1941, fourteen years after the publication of *To the Lighthouse*, her body was found in the River Ouse, her coat pockets filled with stones.

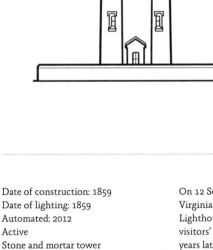

13

Godrevy Lighthouse

Celtic Sea,
Atlantic Ocean
Europe

50° 14′ 33″ N
05° 24′ 01″ W

Date of construction: 1859
Date of lighting: 1859
Automated: 2012
Active
Stone and mortar tower
Height of tower: 26m
Focal height: 37m
Range: 8 n.m.
Current lens: Fresnel, 2nd order
Light characteristic: one white and red
flash at 10-second intervals

On 12 September 1892, a ten-year-old
Virginia Woolf visited the Godrevy
Lighthouse and put her signature in the
visitors' book. A hundred and twenty
years later, the book was sold at auction
by Bonhams for more than £10,000.

14 Great Isaac Cay Lighthouse

THE BERMUDA TRIANGLE is a vaguely defined place, so hazy that it might only be the stuff of myth and imagination. Some of its defenders trace a huge geometric figure over the surface of the Atlantic Ocean and position its points between the Bermuda Islands, Puerto Rico and Miami. They attribute mysterious disappearances to the area and claim that dozens of planes and ships have vanished there like so many puffs of smoke.

SITUATED NEAR THE WESTERNMOST POINT of this so-called Devil's Triangle are the Bimini Islands and, to their north-east, a lighthouse. There, a small reef of sharp coral breaks the surface; a sterile cay, stained with guano, crowned by an imposing iron lighthouse. According to the locals, it's a spot where things happen. Ships sink, maybe for inexplicable reasons or maybe because several different bodies of water meet around it, and the currents of the Great Bahama Bank, the Straits of Florida and the Northwest Providence Channel all lurk together like a pack of subaquatic predators.

The lighthouse is inevitably associated with a number of ghost stories. The most popular, known as 'The Grey Lady', has to do with an unusual sound that can be heard by moonlight. It's said that at the end of the nineteenth century, a ship was wrecked close to the Great Isaac Cay and all those aboard perished. Only a baby survived the disaster. From that moment on, the wails of its anguished mother have crossed the island on nights when the moon is full.

As well as the doubtful apparitions and the spectres wandering around the coral darkness, one real case does remain unsolved. On 4 August 1969, Great Isaac's team of keepers vanished without trace. When anomalies in the light were detected and repeated radio calls went unanswered, a rescue group set off from the Bimini islands. At the lighthouse, they found all the outbuildings in order; tools, clothing and food were in their proper places. However, the lighthouse was totally deserted, and the keepers would never be found.

THE ENIGMA MIGHT HAVE SOMETHING to do with an incident linked to drug-trafficking or the arms trade, or Hurricane Ana might have passed too close to the island on 2 and 3 August and carried the lighthouse-keepers off in the wind, or the disappearance might be related to extraterrestrial abductions, paranormal activity or indeed the cursed vertices of the Bermuda Triangle.

Whether or not this mystery is ever cleared up, there will be no more lighthouse-keepers here. The lighthouse will remain on the reef, upright and hazy like the mast of a ghost ship, while, beside it, the keepers' abandoned homes slowly crumble.

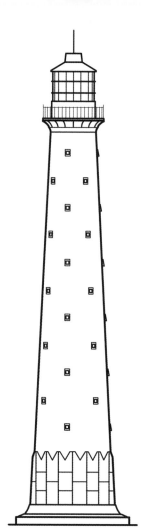

14

Great Isaac Cay Lighthouse

FLORIDA STRAITS,

ATLANTIC OCEAN

AMERICA

26° 02′ 41″ N

79° 05′ 22″ W

Date of construction: 1851
Date of lighting: 1859
Automated: 1969
Deactivated: 2000–2009
Cylindrical tower of cast iron
Height of tower: 46m
Focal height: 54m
Range: 23 n.m.
Light characteristic: one white flash at
15-second intervals

Eight years before it first shone at the
Great Isaac Cay, the lighthouse was
presented at the 1851 Great Exhibition
in London.

You can travel to the cay by boat
from the Bimini islands, though the
lighthouse is closed and it is not
possible to get inside.

4000 m

S T R A I T S
O F
F L O R I D A

East Brother Rock

GREAT ISAAC CAY

West Brother Rock

*Hen and Chicken
Rocks*

Eldorado Shoal

Moselle Bank

B A H A M A S

North Bimini

BIMINI ISLANDS

*nry
ank*

BAHAMAS

Piquet Rocks

Holm Cay

G R E A T   B A H A M A   B A N K

Gun Cay

North Cat Cay

15   Grip Lighthouse

GRIP,
KRISTIANSUND,
NORDMØRE,
MØRE OG
ROMSDAL
(NORWAY)

A FEW MONTHS BEFORE DYING, Edgar Allan Poe wrote his final text. Although this incomplete story had no title, it came to be known as *The Lighthouse*. Written in diary format, only three entries survive. The first begins thus:

JAN 1 — 1796. *This day — my first on the light-house — I make this entry in my Diary, as agreed on with De Grät. As regularly as I can keep the journal, I will — but there is no telling what may happen to a man all alone as I am — I may get sick, or worse . . . So far well! The cutter had a narrow escape — but why dwell on that, since I am here, all safe? My spirits are beginning to revive already, at the mere thought of being — for once in my life at least — thoroughly alone . . .*

THE PLOT UNFOLDS on a remote Norwegian island. The lighthouse and its location do not correspond to any real setting. But forty years after Poe's demise, a lighthouse was constructed on a Norwegian islet that really could have risen out of that writer's imagination.

LIKE A CONSTELLATION OF STARS, an archipelago of tiny islands is scattered across the waters that pummel the Kristiansund coast. On one of them, now uninhabited, you can still visit a fifteenth-century wooden church and walk among the coloured houses of a fishing village. From there, turning one's eyes towards the north, you can make out, on a bare rock, the silhouette of an imposing lighthouse, the second tallest in Norway.

'FOR THIS JOB you need nerves of steel,' warned the advertisement published to recruit lighthouse-keepers for Grip. Even just making landfall on the islet was risky. The dangerous operation, executed with a derrick and a small boat, was a feat worthy of acrobats. The exposed landing place that was used for carrying out these handovers was affectionately called *the circus*. And remaining cooped up in the lighthouse was tougher still. With adverse weather and no chance of building homes on the islet, the lighthouse-keepers' lives were spent mostly in the solitude of the narrow tower itself. Silent men lived alongside the tormenting roar of the diesel engines, a tireless vibration that could be felt from anywhere in the outbuildings.

Svein Jarle Viken, posted to Grip for five years, was barely able to sleep and was assailed by frequent nightmares. In his dreams, Viken was flying over the sea tied to the derrick; he would leave the rock and then land back down on it, over and over again. This anxiety, itself like something out of a story by Poe, persecuted him long after he'd left his isolated lighthouse post.

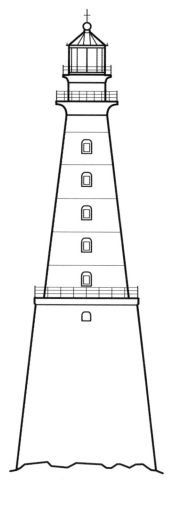

15

Grip Lighthouse

NORWEGIAN SEA,
ATLANTIC OCEAN
EUROPE

63° 14' 01" N
07° 36' 33" E

Date of construction: 1885–88
Date of lighting: 1888
Automated: 1977
Active
Conical cast-iron tower
Height of tower: 44m
Focal height: 47m
Range: 19 n.m.
Light characteristic: white, red and
green light with two eclipses every
8 seconds

A story is told about a woman who
showed up one day at the lighthouse.
With her arrival, an argument broke out
between the two keepers. The tension
grew to be unbearable: there were
chases across the islet, threats with a
knife and an entrenchment inside the
lighthouse. The unfortunate keeper
on whom the door was shut had to
stay out in the open for days until the
fishermen from Grip village came to his
aid. Finally, the authorities resolved to
dismiss the two lighthouse-keepers and
bring the woman back to land.

1000 m

GRIPHØLEN

GRIP

Beksla

Gjevla

Flesa

Kvitingen

Grip

Grøn

Moholmen

Lyngripan

Flatskjelingen

NORGE

KRISTIANSUND

Sveggøya

VIKA   SVEGGEN   *KJERKEVÅGEN*

16   Guardafui Lighthouse

WHEN *THE MUSSOLINI LIGHTHOUSE* was published in 2015, almost nobody in Italy knew what the book was about. Two years earlier, its author, Alberto Alpozzi, hadn't known all that much about lighthouses either. A photographer specializing in crisis zones, he had travelled to the Gulf of Aden for a report about Somali pirates. On his adventure he did not encounter the pirates, but, flying over the far north-east of Somalia in a helicopter, he took photographs of a stone tower that dramatically caught his attention.

CAPE GUARDAFUI MARKS the point of the Horn of Africa. Called Aromatum Promontorium (the promontory of spices) in classical times, and known to the natives as rãs 'Aseyr (the cape of tears), it was named Guardafui (look and flee) by old Italian sailors due to its dangerous currents and its thick and unexpected fogs. Local gangs took advantage of these sudden variations in sea conditions to loot the vessels sailing nearby. They would light bonfires on the cliffs, and the ships, believing the fires to be lighthouses, came closer to the coast, to their misfortune.

EVEN BACK WHEN the Suez Canal first opened in 1869, an idea was already beginning to emerge of illuminating this wild bit of coast which, after colonial disputes, would end up as part of Italian Somaliland. In 1924, a metal-framed tower named the Francesco Crispi Lighthouse was erected on Cape Guardafui, described by the European press of the time as a *forward sentry of Italian civilization on an important maritime route.*

But rebellion against Italian rule was widespread in Somalia, and the lighthouse had to bear attacks on the part of insurgents. The tower was seriously damaged, and the army defending it suffered significant casualties. Following these events, the Italians erected a stone construction reinforced with cement rings; a much hardier structure on which there stands out, as a curious decoration, a huge *fascio littorio* (a stone axe), a symbol of the fascist imperialism then governing Italy.

SOMALIA IS NOT a common holiday destination and Cape Guardafui is an almost inaccessible spot. A changing desert, a treacherous sea and the political instability of the region are allies in defence of its isolation. It is likely that very few Italians, if any at all, have touched this lighthouse's reddish stones in the last seventy years. And though its ruins have thus far survived the passage of time, if it weren't for Alpozzi's photographs, it might remain totally hidden from our view today.

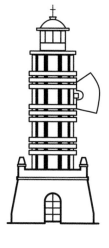

16

Guardafui
Lighthouse

GUARDAFUI

CHANNEL,

INDIAN OCEAN

AFRICA

11° 49′ 00″ N
51° 17′ 00″ E

Date of construction: 1924 and 1930
Date of lighting: 1924 and 1930
Deactivated: 1957
Cylindrical masonry tower
Height of tower: 19m
Focal height: 263m

The last lighthouse-keeper, nicknamed 'The Prince of Guardafui', performed his task until 1957. Antonio Selvaggi had been a prisoner of the English in 1941 and subsequently worked as a barber in Mogadishu. He said in an interview: *We're very isolated, we only have three camels for transport.* Getting to Alula, the nearest town where it was possible to collect the mail, involved two days' travel on the back of one of those animals.

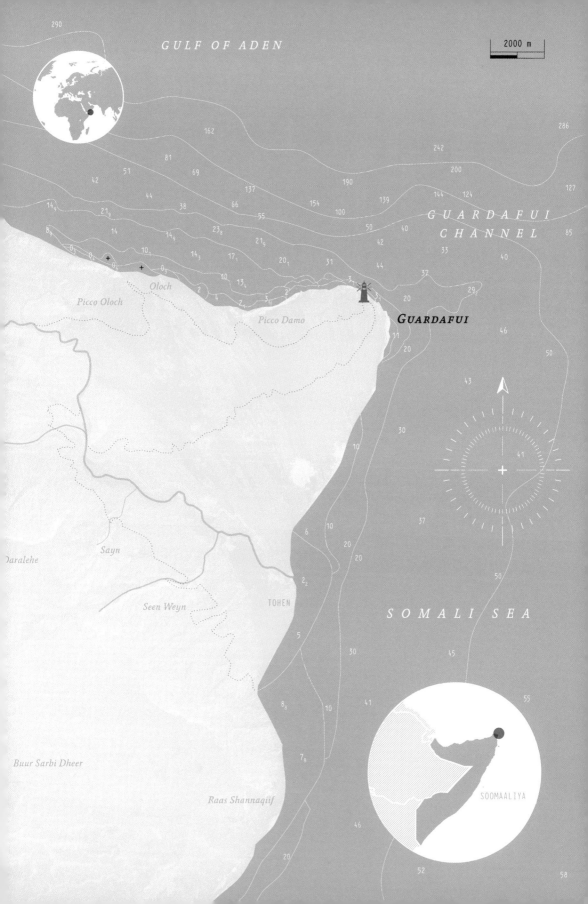

La Jument Lighthouse

Ar Gazec
Rock,
Ouessant
Island,
Finisterre,
Brittany
(France)

Despite the roaring storm, Théodore Malgorn in the lantern room heard the sound of a propeller engine. Curiosity brought him down to the base of the lighthouse. When he opened the door, he spotted a helicopter flying over the rough waters of the Iroise Sea. From the air, the photographer Jean Guichard was watching the insistent way the Atlantic waves struck La Jument. With surprising intuition, he clicked his camera at just the right moment: the lighthouse-keeper standing on the threshold as a giant wave engulfed the tower.

The snapshot leaves the viewer on tenterhooks. Looking at it, you wonder about the picture without knowing what befell the keeper. Perhaps because of the uncertainty that it carried with it, it won a 1990 World Press Photo award. The story of the photo does end happily. The lighthouse-keeper, about to be engulfed by the wave, closed the door in time and escaped to safety. The damage was limited to a scare and some wet feet.

If those were the waves that made La Jument famous, there were others, long before, that had first prompted its construction. The turbulent waters of the Fromveur Passage bore witness to countless shipwrecks, some of them sadly well known, such as that of the English steamer the SS *Drummond Castle*. Charles Eugène Potron, traveller and member of the Paris Geographical Society, survived one of them. After this bitter experience, he bequeathed 400,000 francs in his will for the raising of a lighthouse in the vicinity of the island of Ouessant, and wrote: *Although it is a heroic act to remedy disasters as far as human ability will allow, it is even better to prevent them.* The donor placed just one condition: the work must be completed within seven years of his death.

With some haste, the work began in 1904, and though the lamp did get lit, with great difficulty, within the agreed timeframe, the overly hurried execution meant that in the years that followed, some weaknesses in the tower began to show. The first storms soon revealed anomalous vibrations in the structure. During these storms, the lighthouse-keepers suffered not infrequent moments of panic as the tower threatened to collapse into the sea. Successive attempts were made to restore it, but the work was so complicated and costly that it was thirty years before it was completed. Despite the improvements, La Jument remained, to many people, *the hell of Ouessant.*

After fourteen years of service, Théodore Malgorn departed La Jument in 1991, leaving a lonely, automated lighthouse behind him. He continued to live on the island of Ouessant, wandering its cliffs, glimpsing the imposing silhouette of the tower in the distance and occasionally recalling the moment when a famous wave lashed *the lighthouse of storms.*

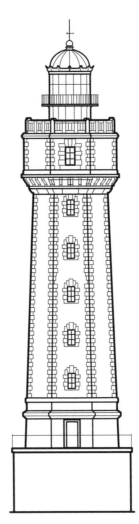

17

La Jument Lighthouse

48° 25′ 40″ N
05° 08′ 00″ W

Date of construction: 1904–11
Date of lighting: 1911
Automated: 1990
Active
Octagonal stone tower
Height of tower: 47m
Focal height: 41m
Range: 22 n.m.
Light characteristic: three red flashes every 15 seconds

In the winter of 2017, the size of the waves striking La Jument was measured. The largest reached a height of over 24.5 metres.

Philippe Lioret's movie, *L'Équipier* (*The Light*), produced in 2004, tells a story set on the island of Ouessant, with the Jument keepers among its characters.

La Jument Lighthouse was designated a French historic monument in December 2015.

1000 m

ÎLE DE KELLER

BAIE DE BENINOU

Le Stiff

BAIE DU STIFF

Men Korn

Créac'h

ÎLE D'OUESSANT

LAMPAUL

PORSGUEN

Pointe de Pern

Nividic

TOULALLAN

PASSAGE DU FROMVEUR

BAIE DE LAMPAUL

Penn ar Viler

BAIE DE PEEN AR ROC'H

Kéréon

Bannec

LA JUMENT

MER D'IROISE

FRANCE

18   Klein Curaçao Lighthouse

OFF THE VENEZUELAN COAST, a small portion of the Netherlands stretches into the south Caribbean Sea. On the island of Curaçao, in the seventeenth century, colonists settled from the Low Countries and the offices of the Dutch West India Company were established, charged with administering the slave trade across much of the Atlantic. The capital, Willemstad, became wealthy thanks to this lucrative activity and today, besides having colonial architecture that's recognized as a World Heritage Site, it is a touristic fiscal paradise.

DUE TO THE NORTH-WESTERLY WINDS and the strong marine currents, ships were frequently wrecked on an island located a couple of hours to the south of Curaçao. On a trip around the windward coast of Klein Curaçao (Little Curaçao), in addition to thousands of plastic bottles and other contemporary junk, you can see the rusty ruins of the oil tanker *Maria Bianca Guidesman* that was wrecked in the 1960s, some remnants of the German freighter *Magdalena* that ran aground here in 1934, and the 2007 remains of the French yacht *Tchao*, which rest on the beach as though it were their graveyard.

THE FIRST LIGHTHOUSE HERE, Prince Hendrik's, was carried off by a hurricane in 1877, before it was thirty years old. The island remained in a state of insecure darkness until 1913, when the light was lit in the tower that still stands today, imposing, in the centre of this solitary place. That lighthouse – pink-hued, like many of Willemstad's buildings – remained active for a while, only to be forgotten as the twentieth century advanced. Its ruin has survived the elements and today it rises up like the ghostly skeleton of one more shipwreck that has made its way inland.

IN THE OPENING DECADE of the twenty-first century, the lighthouse recovered its light in the form of an automated lamp that flashes every fifteen seconds. This was also the same period when the Dutch government expressed its *deep regret and remorse* for the Low Countries' involvement in the international slave trade.

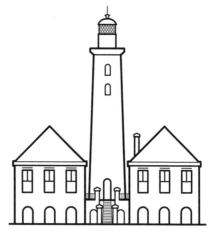

18

Klein Curaçao
Lighthouse

CARIBBEAN SEA
SOUTH AMERICA

11° 59′ 23″ N
68° 38′ 35″ W

Date of construction: 1850 and 1879
Date of lighting: 1850 and 1913
Automated: 2008
Active
Cylindrical masonry tower
Height of tower: 20m
Focal height: 25m
Range: 15 n.m.
Light characteristic: two white flashes
every 15 seconds

In 1871, an English engineer by the name of John Godden started to exploit guano phosphate on Klein Curaçao. Mining and the herds of goats introduced by the settlers led to the desertification of the island's fragile ecosystem.

Although Klein Curaçao is uninhabited, it is possible to get there by boat from Willemstad. You can take an excursion through the lighthouse's surroundings and the former slave quarantine building.

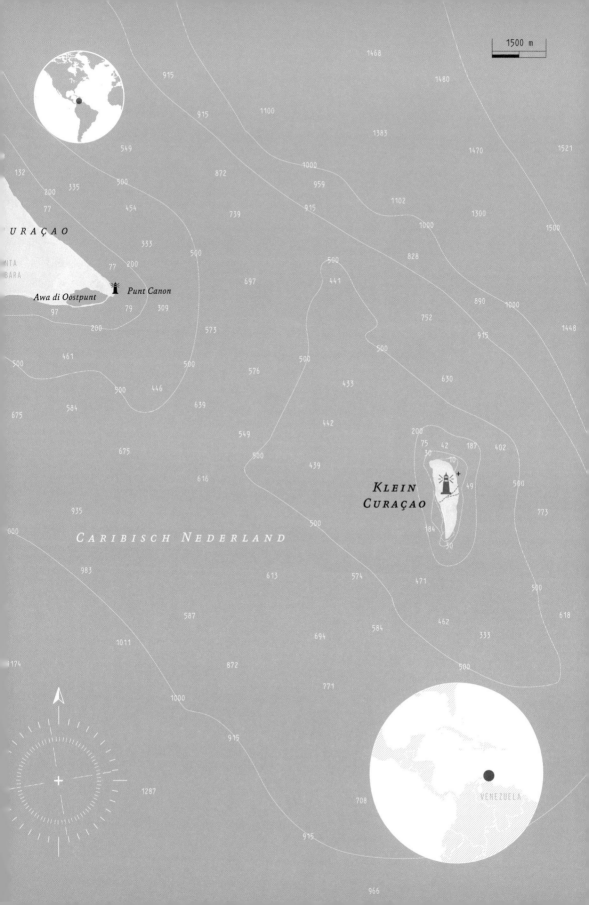

1500 m

1468
1480

915

1383

915   1100

1470   1521

549

1102

1000   1300

872   959

132   335

200   915   828   1500

77   454   1000

739

URAÇAO   333   890   1000

NTA   500
BÁRA   77   200   500   441   752   1448

Awa di Oostpunt   Punt Canon   697   915

97   79   309   500

200   573   500   630

461   576   433   200

500   639   442   75   42   187   402
584   549   30   10

675   500   439   49   500

616   KLEIN   184

935   CURAÇAO   30   773

000   620

983   773

CARIBISCH NEDERLAND   500   574   471   500

587   613   584   462   618

1011   694   333

174   872   771   500

1000

VENEZUELA

915

1287

708

966

Lime Rock Lighthouse

THE FIRST RESCUE occurs on a sombre autumn day. Four young local men are sailing, unconcerned, close to Fort Adams on the Newport coast. One of them climbs the mast and starts to rock back and forth. But what was meant as a joke being played on his friends ends in misfortune. The boat capsizes and the four youths, barely able to swim, struggle desperately to remain afloat. A girl is watching the scene from the lighthouse window. She immediately goes to their aid and, with the help of a small boat, succeeds in getting them to safety. Ida Lewis is just twelve years old.

THE YEAR IS 1858. Five years earlier, her father was named keeper of Lime Rock, a brick building divided into two floors, crowned on its north-west corner with a fixed lamp with a faint white light. This small lighthouse, located around 300 metres from the coast, guides the path of boats towards Newport harbour. When her father suffers a stroke that leaves him incapacitated, Ida and her mother take on the lighthouse's duties. Ida doesn't only take care of the lamp, she also rows daily to take her younger siblings to school. By now she is considered the best swimmer in Newport.

The rescues continued over the years: a sergeant, a soldier, five women . . . Some were carried out in such difficult conditions that Ida needed days to recover from the effort. Aged twenty-seven, with a celebrity status she had never sought, she occupied pages in the most popular magazines of the day, and people would travel to Lime Rock just to meet her. The citizens of Newport gifted her a boat called *Rescue* with gold-plated tholepins and red velvet cushions. Even President Ulysses S. Grant came to visit, and when he got his feet wet attempting to reach the rock, he said: *I have come to see Ida Lewis, and to see her I'd get wet up to my armpits if necessary.*

She quietly married William Wilson and the couple settled at Black Rock Harbour. But her married life did not last long. Ida could not imagine being far from the lighthouse and soon returned to Lime Rock. She was officially named its keeper in 1879. She wrote in her diary:

Sometimes the spray dashes against these windows so thick I can't see out, and for days at a time the waves are so high that no boat would dare come near the rock, not even if we were starving. But I am happy. There's a peace on this rock that you don't get on shore. There are hundreds of boats going in and out of this harbor in summer, and it's part of my happiness to know that they are depending on me to guide them safely.

IT WAS THERE, one October morning in 1911, that Idawalley Zoradia Lewis's light went out for ever. History would remember Lime Rock as Ida Lewis's lighthouse.

19

Lime Rock
Lighthouse

NARRAGANSETT BAY,
ATLANTIC OCEAN
NORTH AMERICA

41° 28′ 40″ N
71° 19′ 35″ W

Date of construction: 1853
Date of lighting: 1854
Automated: 1927
Deactivated: 1963
Brick tower attached to the house
Height of tower: 4m
Focal height: 9.1m
Original lens: Fresnel, 6th order

At the end of the 1920s, a wooden walkway was built to allow access to the rock on foot, and both the residence and the Lime Rock Lighthouse were acquired by a group of seafarers interested in preserving its history. Thus the Ida Lewis Yacht Club was established, and it remains active to this day. Its flag or pennant has a blue lighthouse on a red background and eighteen white stars, representing each of the lives that Ida Lewis saved.

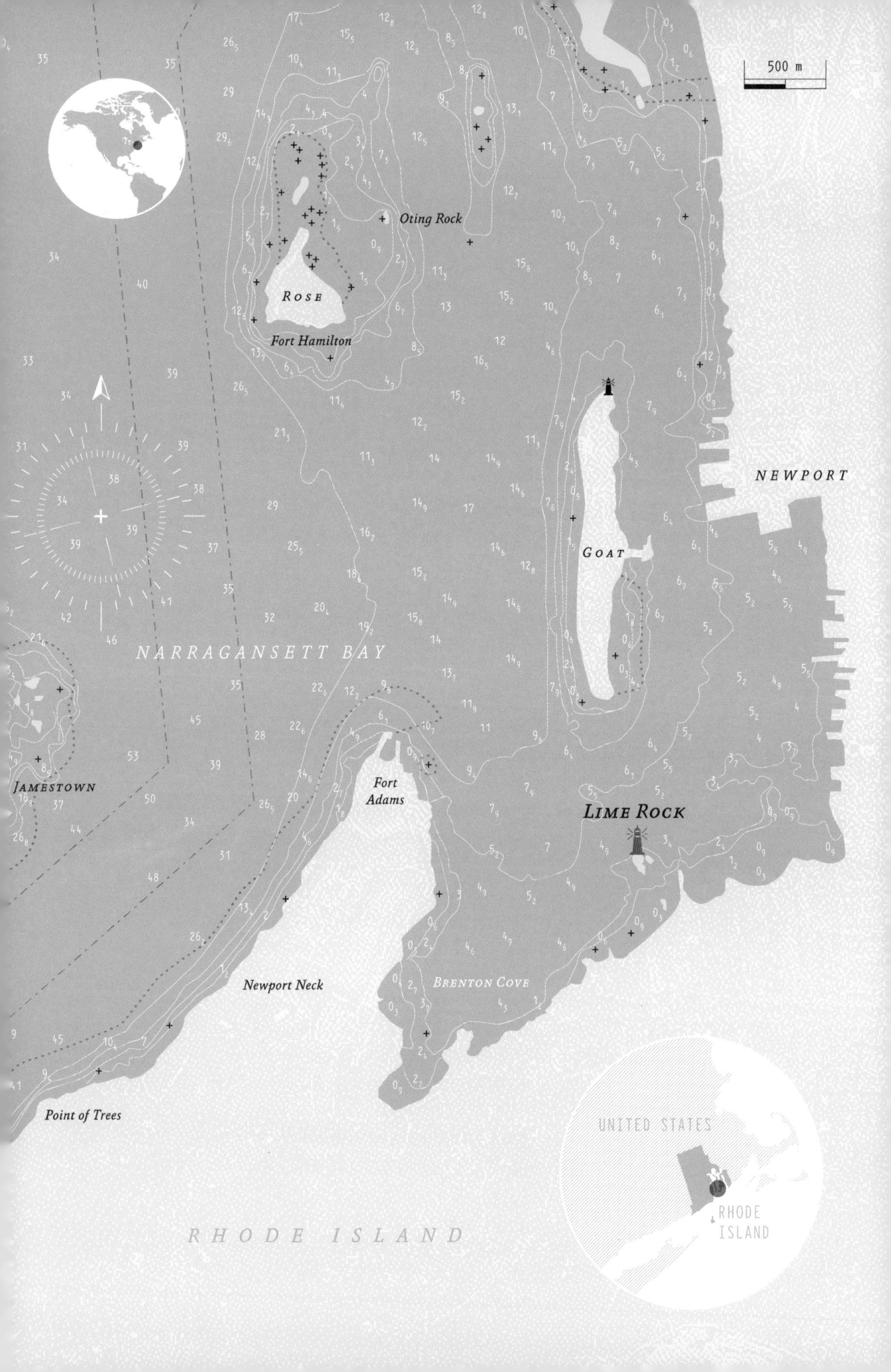

Oting Rock

ROSE

Fort Hamilton

NEWPORT

GOAT

NARRAGANSETT BAY

Jamestown

Fort Adams

LIME ROCK

Newport Neck

BRENTON COVE

Point of Trees

UNITED STATES

RHODE ISLAND

RHODE ISLAND

Longstone Lighthouse

LONGSTONE
ROCK,
FARNE
ISLANDS,
NORTHUM-
BERLAND
(UK)

GRACE DARLING DIED OF tuberculosis at the age of twenty-six. Though she came from a humble family, her remains were laid to rest in a large monument in St Aidan's Church in Bamburgh, her native town, where there is also a museum dedicated to her. It opened its doors a century after the wreck of the SS *Forfarshire*. No photo of Grace survives, but the exhibition gathers together various objects relating to her life, such as a dress she shared with her sister, a lock of hair that has turned white with time and the rowing boat used in the rescue. In another showcase, you can see a children's book written in kanji for Japanese schoolchildren to learn her story.

ON 7 SEPTEMBER 1838, the SS *Forfarshire* split in two. It had left Hull on 5 September and by the following night its engines had failed. At 3 a.m. on the 7th, it smashed against Big Harcar. The Dundee-bound steamer had been surprised by a powerful storm and dragged off course onto the Farne Islands reefs. On board were Captain Humble and his crew, forty passengers and a cargo of cotton and copper.

GRACE WAS WATCHING the storm beat against the lighthouse window. She couldn't sleep that night. With the first light of day she clearly made out the wreckage of a ship and, on a distant islet, shapes that looked human. She told her father, William, the keeper of Longstone, and though it was reckless to take to sea in a storm, they both ventured onto the water in a small coble. They rowed against the tempestuous waters for a whole terrible kilometre. On Big Harcar rock, they found nine battered survivors. Mrs Dawson was holding the lifeless bodies of her two small children, and Reverend Robb, his hands clasped, had just passed away. Grace steered the boat, lashed by the raging waves, bringing it close to the rock while her father assisted the shipwrecked people.

At the same time, a lifeboat with seven men left North Sunderland. But on reaching the wreckage of the *Forfarshire*, they found nobody alive. Exhausted, and considering the challenges of returning to port, they decided first to seek refuge at the Longstone Lighthouse. There, to their surprise, they found the survivors of the disaster together with the Darling family all warming themselves by the fire. The storm stretched on, and nineteen people had to share, over several days, the lighthouse's narrow outbuildings before they could return to shore.

THE NEWS SPREAD like wildfire, and the papers transformed the rescue into a media phenomenon. Grace received tributes, medals and rewards, and the account of her bravery was extolled for posterity.

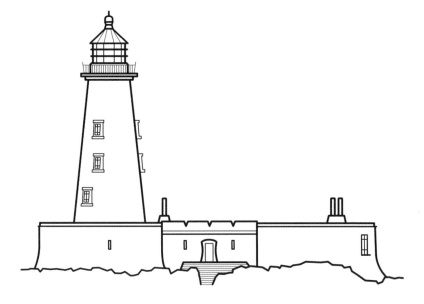

20

Longstone Lighthouse

NORTH SEA,
ATLANTIC OCEAN

EUROPE

55° 38′ 38″ N
01° 36′ 39″ W

Engineer: Joseph Nelson
Date of construction: 1825
Date of lighting: 1826
Automated: 1990
Active
Cylindrical stone tower
Height of tower: 26m
Focal height: 23m
Range: 18 n.m.
Light characteristic: one white flash
at 20-second intervals

Although the Farne Islands are uninhabited, during the Middle Ages they were a place of retreat for monks and hermits. Well-known saints such as St Aidan, St Cuthbert and St Bartholomew of Farne confined themselves there for many years.

Of the six lighthouses that have illuminated these islands since 1773, two remain currently in operation: the Farne Lighthouse (Inner Farne) and the Longstone Lighthouse (Outer Farne).

NORTH SEA

500 m

Longstone

North Wamses

Big Harcar

Brownsman

Staple

STAPLE SOUND

Megstone

Crumstone

FARNE ISLANDS

Solan Rock

Knoxes Reef

The Bush

FARNE SOUND

Inner Farne

INNER SOUND

SEAHOUSES

UNITED KINGDOM

RGH

Maatsuyker Lighthouse

THIS FAR SOUTH, there is no light at all. Just a wild sea and the Roaring Forties. The next piece of land you reach is Antarctica.

Maatsuyker is a large rock detached from Tasmania, caught between the Pacific and Indian Oceans. Wild, unpopulated, inaccessible, some call it South Solitary, though in reality this is the name of an Australian island located 1,600 kilometres further north and closer to human habitation. Maatsuyker is the island of wind, experiencing constant gales of 100 kilometres an hour; and it is the island of water, where it rains at least five days a week. Sometimes the winds howl in fierce storms and are strong enough to knock a person over. They destroy the roof of the lighthouse-keeper's shelter, they break windows and make the tower sway almost until it breaks.

The lightning here is no less notorious than the wind. John Cook, a lighthouse-keeper who served at Maatsuyker for eight years, admitted that the most terrifying moment of his time on the island was when a lightning-bolt hit the tower and the force of the thunder hurled him against the wall. Another bolt that fell in 2015 left the station with no electricity supply for weeks.

Even so, there were also warm and delightful moments for John Cook, when he sighted porpoises and whales, watched the Southern Lights beneath the night sky or marvelled at incomparable sunsets. He wrote in his memoir:

I loved the life of the island, because I knew my body was more alive than it was on the mainland. People asked how we stood the isolation and boredom, but in some ways, it was more stimulating to have your senses turned up.

WHEN THE LIGHTHOUSE was installed in 1891, the only way of communicating with the outside world in the case of an emergency was by messenger pigeons. They were sent to Hobart three at a time in the hope that at least one of them would reach its target. And the work was hard. Climbing one hundred and twenty steps up to the lantern, lighting the kerosene lamps, pumping gas every twenty minutes to secure a light that was immaculate and powerful. This task went on through every night until the lighthouse was electrified and its lamps changed. Since then, southern Tasmanian fishing boats have been guided by a much sadder light. According to Cook, this was the *beginning of the end*. The arrival of electricity would add lighthouse-keeper to the list of trades under threat of extinction.

JOHN COOK PUBLISHED HIS MEMOIRS under the title *The Last Lighthouse Keeper*. At the age of eighty-five, his blue eyes are still seeking out horizons. In his will, he has requested one thing: that he might rest on Maatsuyker for all eternity.

21

**Maatsuyker
Lighthouse**

PACIFIC AND
INDIAN OCEAN
OCEANIA

43° 39′ 25″ S
146° 16′ 17″ E

Date of construction: 1891
Date of lighting: 1891
Automated: 1996
Active
Conical brick tower
Height of tower: 15m
Focal height: 140m
Range: 26 n.m.
Light characteristic: one white flash at
7.5-second intervals, with one flash in
four omitted

The original lighthouse was replaced
in 1996. Although the new lighthouse
is automated with solar power, in
recent years a volunteer programme
has been in place for a couple to
spend six months living on the island.
The temporary tenants commit to
carrying out the tasks of watching and
maintaining the facilities and taking
meteorological readings. In the first
call, the Tasmanian authorities received
more than a thousand applications.

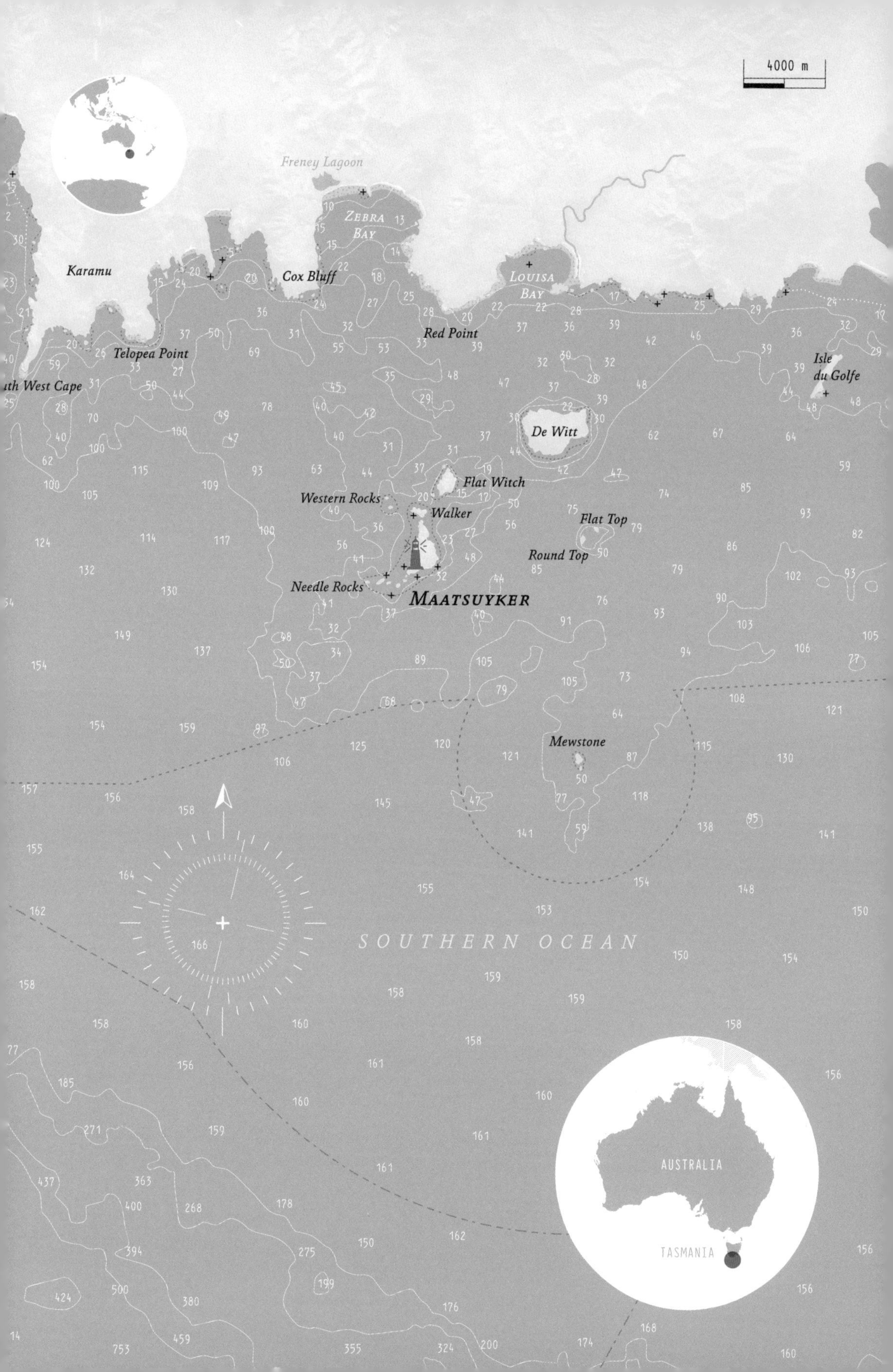

4000 m

Freney Lagoon

Karamu

ZEBRA BAY

Cox Bluff

LOUISA BAY

Red Point

uth West Cape

Telopea Point

Isle du Golfe

De Witt

Flat Witch

Western Rocks

Walker

Flat Top

Round Top

Needle Rocks

MAATSUYKER

Mewstone

SOUTHERN OCEAN

AUSTRALIA

TASMANIA

Matinicus Rock Lighthouse

IN THE 1970S, when the inexperienced Kevin Arsenault was appointed assistant keeper at the Matinicus Lighthouse, about which he knew barely a thing, he asked his colleagues in the coast guard what life there was like. One of them assured him that there was a young woman waiting behind every tree.

If Arsenault had read the Lighthouse Board annual report of 1891, he would have known that on Matinicus Rock *there is neither tree nor shrub, and hardly a blade of grass ... The surface is rough and irregular and resembles a confused pile of loose stone. Portions of the rock are frequently swept over by waves which move the huge boulders into new positions.*

And indeed, on the wild island there were more lighthouses thriving than plants, since a pair of twin towers had been raised up at its ends to illuminate the most dangerous waters of Maine.

BUT THERE REALLY HAD been women on Matinicus Rock, and if they were remarkable for anything it was for their boldness and courage. Abbie Burgess arrived, aged thirteen, in the company of her parents and her little sisters. Abbie would help her father Samuel, who was charged with looking after the lighthouse, in the duties of maintaining the lamp, and she would take care of her mother, who had been incapacitated by illness.

In January 1856, Samuel Burgess went off in a boat to fetch provisions. While he was away, a storm rose up suddenly, preventing his return. After three days, the winds picked up strength and the sea grew ever choppier until a large part of the island was underwater. When the house they lived in was flooded, Abbie moved her mother and sisters to the only place that was safe for taking refuge: the north tower. With the water up to her knees, she ventured out to rescue the hens that were still in the yard. She managed to save all but one. Moments later, a terrible wave hit the island and carried away the family's home and the henhouse. Unable to leave the lighthouse for four weeks, they survived on a daily ration of one cup of maize and an egg. All the while, Abbie kept the lamps lit. Finally, the storm abated. Samuel Burgess returned to the island in great distress at the thought he would not see his family again. However, there was a happy reunion when he found everybody safe and sound.

FIVE YEARS LATER, Matinicus Rock would have a new lighthouse-keeper: John Grant arrived with his son Isaac to tend to the island's lamp. The Burgess family had to move away, but Abbie remained a while at the lighthouse to teach its workings to the newly arrived keepers. A romance quickly blossomed between Abbie and Isaac that was as impulsive as the Atlantic swell. Abbie would not be leaving after all. The couple married the following year. Four children were born, who grew up among the implacable winds.

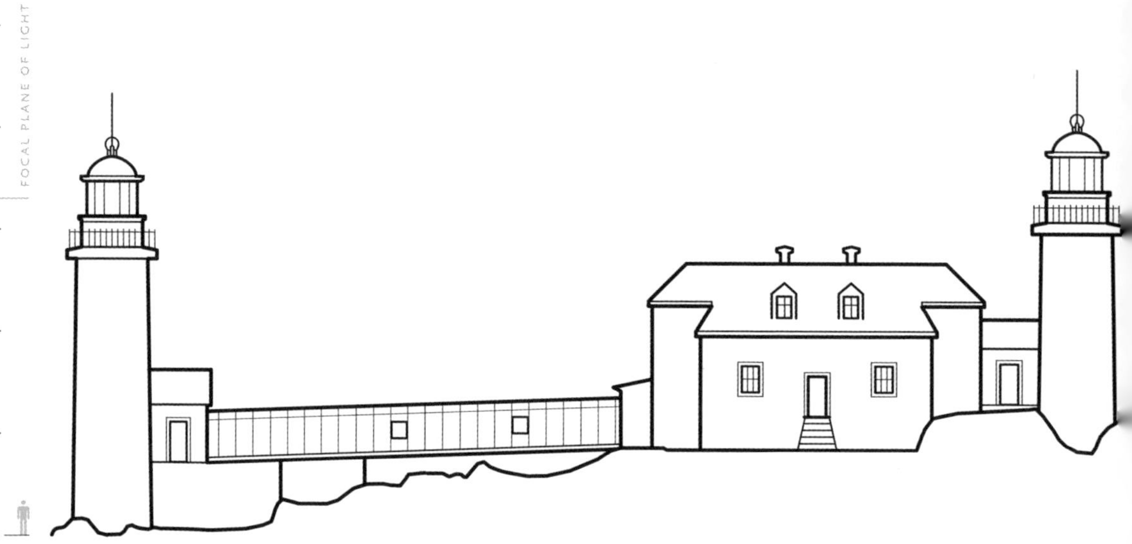

22

Matinicus Rock Lighthouse

ATLANTIC OCEAN

NORTH AMERICA

43° 47' 05" N
68° 51' 18" W

Engineer: Alexander Parris
Date of construction: 1827
Date of lighting: 1846
Automated: 1983
Active
Cylindrical granite towers
Height of towers: 14.5m
Focal height: 27m
Range: 20 n.m.
Light characteristic: one white flash at
10-second intervals

Abbie Burgess died in 1892. In her final letter, she wrote that she frequently dreamed about the old Matinicus Rock lamps and wondered whether her soul would continue to take care of the lighthouse even after it had left her exhausted body.

The lighthouse was added to the US National Register of Historic Places in 1988.

No Mans Land

MATINICUS

Wheaton

Tenpound

RAGGED

WOODEN BALL

ATLANTIC OCEAN

MATINICUS ROCK

1000 m

MAINE

UNITED
STATES

Navassa Lighthouse

AT THE START OF the nineteenth century, guano was a much-sought-after raw material. This organic manure, produced by the vast accumulation of sea-bird deposits, proved an effective fertilizer for the intensive farming that was rapidly growing then. It is not hard to understand the sudden interest in the hundreds of small islands, islets, rocks and cays that, over thousands of years, had been buried under the excrement of albatrosses, cormorants, gannets and seagulls.

In 1856, the US Congress granted its citizens legal authorization to take possession of any guano-containing island that was not under the jurisdiction of any other country. In the second half of the nineteenth century, more than a hundred islands would be occupied in the name of the Guano Islands Act.

TWO BOATS DESPATCHED BY Christopher Columbus from Jamaica to Hispaniola stumbled across a nondescript island and, though they went right past because it was *all rock and there was no fresh water on it, or any trees, but only rocks,* they christened it Navassa. Sailors avoided landing there for the next three hundred years until, in 1857, Peter Duncan, a US captain, staked a claim for the island. Navassa contained a million tons of guano.

One hundred and forty African-American labourers from Maryland were tasked with exploiting the fertilizer, under the iron control of their white overseers and the harsh tropical sun. In 1889, a mutiny broke out among the workers, and five foremen were violently killed. The ringleaders were tried and convicted in Baltimore. After the revolt, the exploitation of guano went into decline until, right in the middle of the Cuban War, the phosphate company filed for bankruptcy.

THE ISLAND remained uninhabited, and thereafter was only frequented after the opening of the Panama Canal, when the Windward Passage turned out to be the fastest navigational route from the US east coast to the Pacific. Then a large concrete lighthouse was erected, almost 50 metres tall, with a few out-buildings to house its keepers. For fifteen years, the station was tended by lighthouse-keepers from the US Coast Guard. But nobody survived the suffocating heat of this remote place for long. In 1929, the engineer George R. Putnam developed a system that would allow the light to operate self-sufficiently, and Navassa became one of the first automated lighthouses in the world.

The light fell silent in 1996. Since then, wild cats, dogs and pigs wander around the gigantic tower. Fig-trees and scrubland grow uncontrolled on the forgotten ground. A vast landmark highlights the lush tropical weeds that are ruthlessly taking possession of the island.

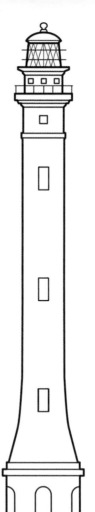

23

Navassa
Lighthouse

CARIBBEAN SEA

CENTRAL AMERICA

18° 24′ 01″ N
75° 00′ 39″ W

Date of construction: 1917
Date of lighting: 1917
Automated: 1929
Deactivated: 1996
Concrete tower with stone base
Height of tower: 49.3m
Focal height: 120m
Original lens: Fresnel, 2nd order

Navassa has been disputed territory for over two hundred years. Although it was the first island occupied by the United States following the 1856 Guano Islands Act, it had already been officially claimed by Haiti in 1804. Currently, and in spite of the dispute, the island is managed by the US Fish and Wildlife Service.

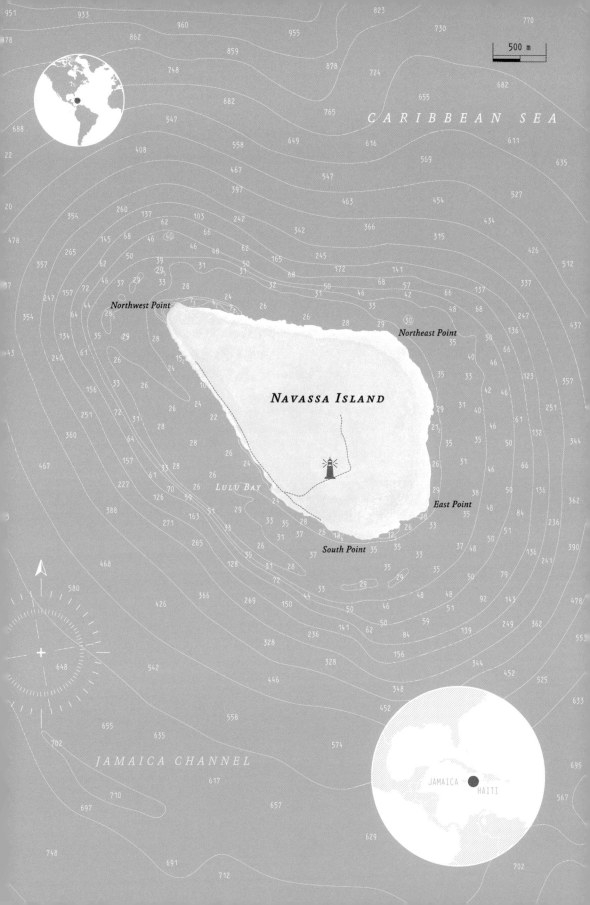

CARIBBEAN SEA

NAVASSA ISLAND

Northwest Point

Northeast Point

LULU BAY

East Point

South Point

JAMAICA CHANNEL

JAMAICA   HAITI

500 m

Robben Island Lighthouse

As a memento of his time on Robben Island, Nelson Mandela produced a series of coloured sketches. The drawings represent the places that remained in his memory: *the harbour, the church, the window, the lighthouse and the cell.*

The island of seals – *robben* in Dutch – is a piece of African land that 12,000 years ago ventured into the ocean. Some ships laden with treasure were wrecked on its coasts, and from the dawn of the European colonialization of South Africa, bonfires were lit at its highest point to warn ships of the need to skirt around it. There, Jan van Riebeeck, promoter of wine production, the fur trade, and the slave trade, and Cape Town administrator, raised the first lighthouse on South African soil in 1657. And although it quickly succumbed to storms, the light from the tower built by Joseph Flack in 1864 remains alive to this day.

Lighthouses, islands and prisons have often been united by rather grim links. The Dutch, besides installing a beacon on Robben, found it a suitable place for exiling *unwanted citizens.* Many leaders of anticolonial movements ended up as bones on that island. Later, under British rule, the cruel prison was joined by a leper colony and a mental hospital. For almost a century, the colony housed hundreds of patients, while the penitentiary extended its railings and strengthened its walls.

Lighthouse-keepers and prison guards had a close relationship. The tower men and their families depended on the penitentiary services for the supply of goods and provisions. The guards, who were likewise detained on the island for a good part of their time, spent their free hours at the foot of the lighthouse and several ended up marrying lighthouse-keepers' daughters.

Mandela himself arrived on Robben Island in the winter of 1964 and spent the next eighteen years locked up in a four-square-metre cell. He had a bucket for a toilet, from 6 a.m. he worked in a quarry that left him almost blind, and in a single year he was only able to receive two letters and one thirty-minute visit. The maximum-security prison where he was incarcerated with other political activists was one of the most ruthless examples of racial suppression during South Africa's apartheid era.

Lit by an intermittent light, Nelson Mandela, Walter Sisulu, Govan Mbeki and Ahmed Kathrada combined their determination to fight against oppression. There, held in detention, they forged their leadership, not knowing that they would become the heroes who would guide South Africa's destiny.

24

Robben Island Lighthouse

Atlantic Ocean

Africa

38° 48′ 52″ S
18° 22′ 29″ E

Engineer: Joseph Flack
Date of construction: 1865
Date of lighting: 1865
Active
Cylindrical masonry tower
Height of tower: 18m
Focal height: 30m
Range: 24 n.m.
Light characteristic: intermittent red flashing of 5-second duration every 7 seconds

Robben Island was declared a World Heritage Site by UNESCO, the United Nations Educational, Scientific and Cultural Organisation, in 1999. The former prison today houses a museum dedicated to the memory of the victims of apartheid. Some of the old political prisoners work there and recount their experiences from their lives on Robben Island to the visitors.

Rocher aux Oiseaux Lighthouse

Rocher aux
Oiseaux
(Bird Rock),
Madeleine
Islands,
Quebec
(Canada)

THE NATURALIST John James Audubon was sailing 30 kilometres from the Madeleine archipelago, islands where the loss of ships was such a frequent occurrence that much of the population had the surnames of wrecks and their houses had been built from wreckage. He spotted an isolated crag with reddish cliffs speckled with small, pale marks. When he got close enough, an infinite number of white dots took flight and blocked out the sky, as if a sudden snowstorm had been unleashed. Thousands of seabirds were welcoming him to the Rocher aux Oiseaux: Bird Rock.

A BEACON WAS ESTABLISHED there in 1870, and Peter Mitchell, Minister of Marine and Fisheries, declared: *I feel much pleasure in stating that at . . . the most difficult place in the Dominion on which to erect a lighthouse, owing to the surf which continually breaks around it . . . the efforts of the Department have been entirely successful in erecting the lighthouse and buildings in connection therewith.*

THE LIGHT SHONE, and an ill omen was born. The first lighthouse-keeper, Jacques Guitte, having disembarked on the rock, tendered his resignation, warning: *No man will keep this lighthouse for more than ten years without meeting misfortune.* The passage of time confirmed this premonition with the following chronology. 1872: after some months of solitary work, keeper George Preston leaves the lighthouse strapped into a straitjacket. 1880: keeper Peter Whalen and his son freeze to death just a few kilometres from the lighthouse. The previous day they went out to sea to hunt seals. Miraculously, Thivierge, his assistant, survives. 1881: on a foggy day, keeper Charles Chiasson is blown up on firing the fog cannon. His son and a friend also die in the accident. 1891: lighthouse-keeper Télesphore Turbide loses an arm operating the same cannon. 1897: on a frozen sea, keeper Arsène Turbide manages to walk 90 kilometres to Cape Breton. He and two other men left the lighthouse three days earlier to hunt seals but got caught in a storm. He dies after two weeks of agony. His cousin Charles and assistant keeper Cormier are never found. 1897: in a night of poor visibility, assistant keeper Melanson is gravely injured firing a flare gun. 1911: keeper Wilfred Bourque takes his shotgun and goes out to look for ducks. Hours later, his lifeless body is found floating just off the island. 1922: Albin Bourque and his two assistants suddenly fall ill. Albin dies on his way to hospital; one assistant follows eighteen months later, and the other survives with life-changing after-effects. The water tank had been contaminated with bird excrement.

In 1955, lighthouse-keeper Alfred Arsenault retires happily from the post after more than twelve years in charge of the lighthouse without any tragedy befalling him. When asked if the prophecy worried him, he shrugs.

25

**Rocher aux
Oiseaux
Lighthouse**

GULF OF SAINT
LAWRENCE,
ATLANTIC OCEAN
NORTH AMERICA

47° 50′ 17″ N
61° 08′ 44″ W

Date of construction: 1870–1887–1967
Date of lighting: 1870
Automated: 1987
Deactivated: 2011
Wood and concrete tower
Height of tower: 15.2m
Focal height: 49m
Range: 21 n.m.

Captain Jacques Cartier named the
desolate islet the Rocher aux Margaulx
– the Rock of Gannets – when he was
sailing the Gulf of Saint Lawrence
in 1535 in search of the Northwest
Passage.

The only way to reach the base of the
lighthouse is via a 147-step staircase
located at the northern cliff.

Today, the rock is a refuge for
migratory birds, and a protected
Canadian marine sanctuary.

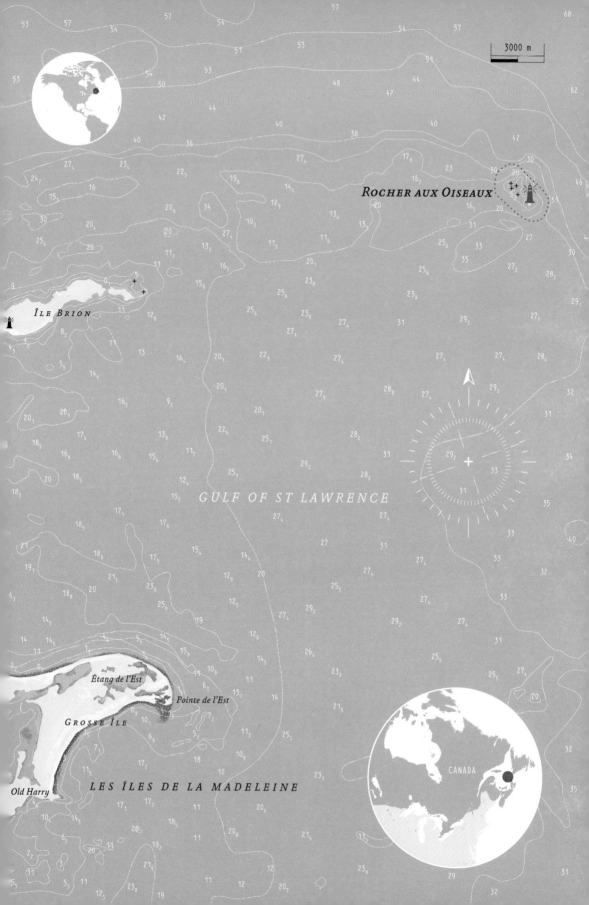

ROCHER AUX OISEAUX

ÎLE BRION

GULF OF ST LAWRENCE

3000 m

CANADA

Étang de l'Est

Pointe de l'Est

GROSSE ÎLE

Old Harry

LES ÎLES DE LA MADELEINE

26 Rubjerg Knude Lighthouse

RUBJERG,
HJØRRING,
JUTLAND
(DENMARK)

THE DUNE SHIFTS SLOWLY and so silently that it might swallow up the tower without meeting any resistance and bury it beneath a cloak of golden particles. A photo shows a lighthouse assailed by the sand in a scene from another age, something out of ancient Egypt. A place besieged not by the waters, but by the land. You would never guess this desert landscape is a Nordic country in the twenty-first century.

A hundred years before this photograph was taken, the Danish coast of Vendsyssel-Thy – at a point 60 metres above sea level and 200 metres from the coast – witnessed the erection of the Rubjerg Knude Lighthouse.

THE LIGHT CONTINUED to guide ships, while the winds and the sea pushed the sands from the beach inland. Bit by bit, a dune grew, and its shadow loomed over the lighthouse. To prevent its advance, a wooden barrier was erected and grasses and bushes planted around it. The measures were useless; in 1968, the dune blocked the light from the sea. Twelve years later – with the lighthouse now no longer in operation and with the intention of boosting the area as a tourist destination – a large quantity of sand was removed and a museum with a café opened in the adjacent buildings. Making a vain attempt to deceive nature, the complex operated for a time, but it was finally abandoned in 2002. The dune had progressed, relentless, onto the facilities, bringing down roofs and breaking the buildings. Only the tower managed to survive the determination of the sand, and, patiently awaiting its burial, it has remained standing for another two decades.

BEHIND THE DUNE, an unsettled sea was approaching, with its incessant need to conquer coastal territory. With the cliffs eroded, when the waters were just metres from the lighthouse and everything foreshadowed that it would collapse onto the beach, the light fled inland.

In a complicated intervention, the Rubjerg Knude Lighthouse was transported 70 metres inland on rails, using a complex system of hydraulics. Thousands of people were present for the operation – tourists, curious bystanders, journalists, labourers – and it was broadcast by Danish television onto various channels around the world. The feat, in its one minute of media glory, came across like a commercial: ten weeks of planning. Seven hundred and twenty tonnes shifted. A six-hour journey. An average speed of 12 metres per hour. More than five million Danish kroner.

But the titanic effort of those human beings to save the structure will be fleeting in the face of nature's stubborn power. In the best-case scenario, it will grant the old Rubjerg Knude Lighthouse another forty years of life.

26

Rubjerg Knude Lighthouse

North Sea,
Atlantic Ocean
Europe

57° 26' 56" N
09° 46' 28" E

Date of construction: 1899
Date of lighting: 1900
Deactivated: 1968
Square masonry tower
Height of tower: 23m
Focal height: 90m
Range: 18 n.m.

The lighthouse's original optic was produced by a French firm, Barbier & Bénard.

The master mason Kjeld Pedersen from Lønstrup was responsible for moving the tower on 22 October 2019.

Rubjerg Knude is not what you'd call an isolated spot. The lighthouse attracts more than 250,000 visitors a year.

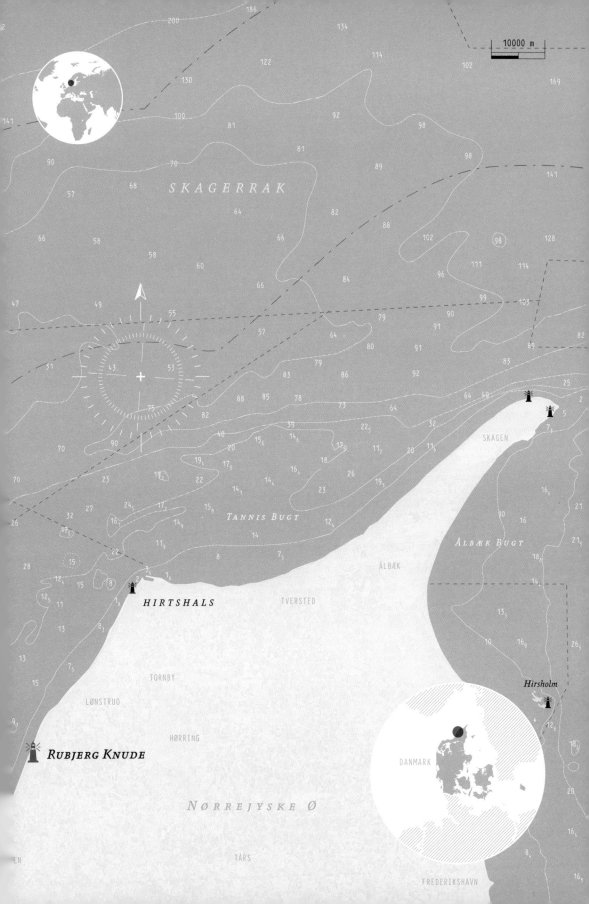

27   San Juan de Salvamento Lighthouse

ISLA DE
LOS ESTADOS,
PATAGONIA
(ARGENTINA)

TRAVEL COMPANIES in Argentine Patagonia advertise excursions to visit the *Lighthouse at the End of the World*, though the truth is their boats only get as far as the Les Éclaireurs Lighthouse. This visit offers the tourist a picturesque setting in the Beagle Channel, but the real gem is found further east, beyond the edges of the Isla Grande de Tierra del Fuego. It was this small lighthouse situated 13,000 kilometres from Amiens, the French city where Jules Verne was living, that inspired the writer to create one of his last novels, *The Lighthouse at the End of the World*.

THE YEAR 1884 saw the establishment on the uninhabited Isla de los Estados of a sub-prefecture, a military prison, a rescue station and the first lighthouse to be constructed on Argentine soil. The San Juan de Salvamento Lighthouse consisted of a modest wooden house, six metres tall. Its weak light did not provide very good visibility since clouds would often perch over the island concealing the lighthouse. Perhaps for this reason, the Argentine government decided to erect another, called Año Nuevo, on Isla Observatorio, located further north and less exposed to the rigours of the southern-latitude climate. The lamp at San Juan de Salvamento remained lit until October 1902, three years before the posthumous publication of Jules Verne's novel.

AMID A SNOWSTORM and a sea lashed by the Furious Fifties – the implacable Antarctic winds – an insignificant kayak finds itself adrift opposite the cliffs of the Isla de los Estados. The French adventurer André Bronner sends out a prayer to appease the elements and swears that if he survives the storm, he will return to this place one day. Two years later, in 1995, he keeps his promise and spends months on the island in lonely isolation, with just the barest survival equipment. Sitting on the ruins of the old lighthouse and fascinated by Verne's tale, a dream begins to take shape: the project to rebuild the lighthouse at the End of the World.

TODAY THERE ARE three identical lighthouses positioned in different parts of the globe. One on the Isla de los Estados, built by Bronner in 1998 at the original San Juan Cape location, from parts made in France. Another on France's Atlantic coast, erected on pillars, opposite the city of La Rochelle, Bronner's birthplace. And finally, alongside some remains of the original lighthouse, you can see a life-size model at the Maritime Museum of Ushuaia. Just metres from this lighthouse at the End of the World, in a display case in the library, is one of just two surviving first editions of Jules Verne's novel.

27

San Juan de Salvamento Lighthouse

ATLANTIC OCEAN

SOUTH AMERICA

54° 43′ 56″ S

63° 51′ 25″ W

Date of construction: 1884
Date of lighting: 1884
Deactivated: 1902
Rebuilt: 1998
Automated: 1998
Active
Octagonal wooden tower
Height of tower: 6.5m
Focal height: 70m
Light characteristic: two white flashes of 3 seconds every 15 seconds

Ten years before the birth of the San Juan Lighthouse, the Argentine sailor Luis Piedrabuena built a shelter nearby to help ships in danger of wreck. He managed to save 146 people.

In *La Australia Argentina* (1898), the writer Roberto J. Payró describes the Isla de los Estados, or Chuanisin – the island of abundance in the language of the native Patagonians – as a natural prison and a ship graveyard.

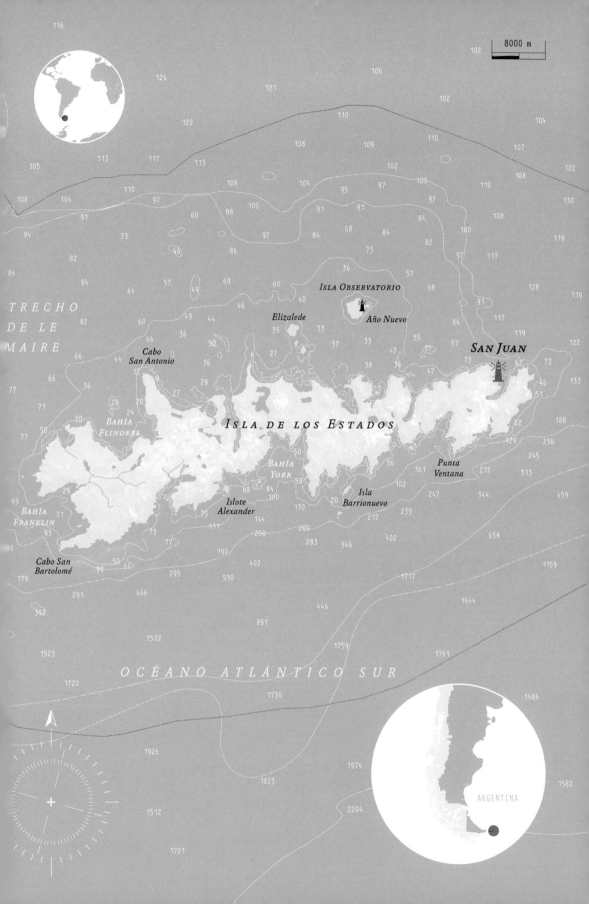

8000 m

ESTRECHO DE LE MAIRE

Isla Observatorio

Elizalede

Año Nuevo

SAN JUAN

Cabo San Antonio

ISLA DE LOS ESTADOS

Bahía Flinders

Bahía York

Punta Ventana

Islote Alexander

Isla Barrionuevo

Bahía Franklin

Cabo San Bartolomé

OCÉANO ATLÁNTICO SUR

ARGENTINA

Smalls Lighthouse

ON THE SNAKING WATERS OF WALES, there was once a lighthouse built with all the delicacy one would more usually employ for making a violin. Henry Whiteside, maker of musical instruments in Liverpool, placed a lamp supported on nine oak columns onto a rock, in such a way that the waves would pass through its structure to die 30 kilometres further on, when they touched the coast.

In 1777, when the works were nearly done, the luthier was himself caught at the lighthouse, trapped there by intense gales. With hardly any water and no supplies, and perhaps while playing on the melancholy strings of his violin, he threw three bottles into the sea with a desperate message: *Sir, being now in a most dangerous and distressed condition upon the Smalls, do hereby trust Providence will bring to your hand this, which prayeth for your immediate assistance to fetch us off the Smalls before the next spring or we fear we shall all perish . . .*

To his good fortune, at least one of the bottles was found in time, and he could be rescued before his confinement ended in tragedy.

THE ISOLATION SUFFERED by the Smalls lighthouse-keepers was so extreme that twenty years later another misfortune occurred. One day in 1801, the distress signal was raised over the tower. But for four months, a protracted storm prevented any help. On the coast, the keepers' families were left in great anguish, and, night after night, they approached the Pembrokeshire cliffs to scan the horizon. The distress flag remained raised, but the light never failed to shine.

The only people at the lighthouse were the keepers Thomas Griffith and Thomas Howell, who were well known to argue.

Griffith had died in unclear circumstances. And Howell, who had tried to help him, had a dilemma: if he tossed the body into the sea, he would likely be accused of murder. So he constructed an improvised coffin for his companion and placed it in a corner of the room. While waiting for the rescue boat, Howell shared the room with the deceased for several days, but when the stench of decomposition became unbearable, he tied the box up with some ropes and moved it outside. Lashed by the gales and beating constantly against the light-house, the wood of the coffin gave way. Griffith, like a contortionist, was left caught between the ropes with half his body outside the coffin. Howell closed his eyes but couldn't help witnessing the grim scene: the corpse's hand, swaying in the wind, seemed to be waving at him.

Finally, after some torturous weeks, Howell was saved. His mental and physical state upon reaching the land was so pitiful that some of his relatives could not recognize him. It is said that Howell never went near another light-house again.

28

Smalls Lighthouse

Celtic Sea,
Atlantic Ocean
Europe

51° 43′ 16″ N
05° 40′ 11″ W

Engineers: Henry Whiteside (1776) and
James Walker (1861)
Date of construction (first lighthouse):
1776
Date of construction (current): 1861
Automated: 1987
Active
Cylindrical stone tower
Height of tower: 41m
Focal height: 36m
Range: 18 n.m.
Light characteristic: three white flashes
every 15 seconds

The current lighthouse was built under
the direction of James Walker, using a
design based on the Eddystone Tower.
In 1978, a helipad was added atop the
lamp, and the lamp itself was automated
in 1987.

The Smalls tragedy has inspired several
contemporary cinematic works. Chris
Crow's *The Lighthouse* (2016) is based
on the story of Griffith and Howell,
and Robert Eggers, who directed *The
Lighthouse* (2019), wrote his screenplay
after researching the incident at the
Welsh lighthouse.

Stannard Rock Lighthouse

STANNARD
ROCK, LAKE
SUPERIOR,
MARQUETTE,
MICHIGAN
(USA)

THE LONELIEST LIGHTHOUSE in North America has never touched the sea. It has withstood nine-metre waves, ice sheets over three metres thick, and winds so strong they forced the keepers to tie themselves down with ropes so as not to be blown away. But its light has never illuminated anything but fresh water.

In the middle of Lake Superior – an area as big as Austria – lurks an underwater mountain. It only emerges a metre from the surface, more than 40 kilometres from anywhere. In 1835, Captain Charles Stannard came across it unexpectedly and was shaken by fear as though he'd met a ghost. Years later, when the trade routes spread across the Great Lakes, a light was lit there to draw attention to the hazard. It was a difficult and costly achievement; twenty years of debate and another five of work were needed to get the lighthouse completed.

ON STANNARD ROCK, the calendar proceeds at its own pace. Keeper Edward Chambers and his three assistants didn't learn of Theodore Roosevelt's victory in the 1904 presidential elections until five weeks later. That same winter, the boat due to transport them to land was delayed a month by the ice. By the time it reached Stannard Rock, the four men, desperate and out of provisions, were getting ready to set off on a suicide journey in a small boat across the frozen lake. Years later, a radio station was installed on the rock, which managed to mitigate the lighthouse-keepers' homesickness. The short-waves raised a bridge of words over the water to their fellows at the Marquette lighthouse. These other keepers, located on the land, would read to those isolated on the rock: letters from their wives, telegrams from the coast guard and newspaper articles that kept them close to the world.

A TRAGIC OCCURRENCE marked Stannard Rock's transformation. On the night of 18 June 1961, a terrible explosion, fed by 4,000 litres of petrol and propane, shook the lighthouse's stores. Walter Scobie had been asleep at the time on the upper floor and was blown clear off his bunk. Oscar Daniel, a maintenance worker who had arrived the previous day, was trapped under a door. Richard Horne, seeing the lifeboat adrift, hurled himself into the water to try, without success, to retrieve it. The lighthouse-keeper William Maxwell had the worst luck of all and died instantly. The icebreaker *Woodrush* managed to reach the lighthouse three days later. The rescuers couldn't access the tower itself owing to the thick smoke, but they found three men huddled under a tarpaulin. The keepers had survived thanks to a jar of ketchup and two tins of beans.

Although the lighthouse was repaired, nobody would live on Stannard Rock again. The loneliest lighthouse in North America became even more desolate.

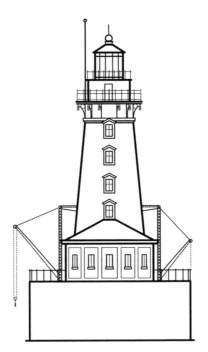

29

Stannard Rock Lighthouse

LAKE SUPERIOR

NORTH AMERICA

47° 11′ 00″ N
87° 13′ 30″ W

Engineer: Orlando Metcalfe Poe
Date of construction: 1877–83
Date of lighting: 1883
Automated: 1962
Active
Limestone tower
Height of tower: 30m
Focal height: 31m
Range: 18 n.m.
Light characteristic: one white flash at 6-second intervals

The long-service record at Stannard Rock belongs to Elmer Sormunen, who fulfilled his role as assistant for twenty-one straight years, until his retirement in 1957.

Working as a keeper at Stannard Rock was dangerous, but it did at least have the occasional benefit. The reef is one of the best places in America for trout-fishing.

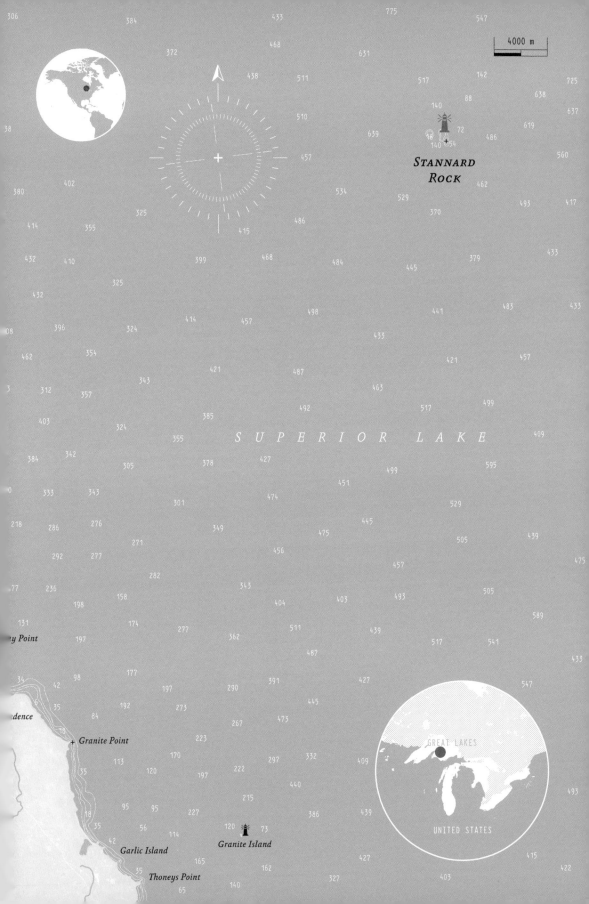

4000 m

STANNARD
ROCK

S U P E R I O R   L A K E

GREAT LAKES

UNITED STATES

Granite Point

Garlic Island

Thoneys Point

Granite Island

Stephens Island Lighthouse

Takapourewa
or Stephens
Island,
Marlborough
(New
Zealand)

David Lyall liked being alone. When he was notified that he had been appointed to the post of assistant lighthouse-keeper on an uninhabited island, he smiled. With his lifelong interest in nature, he imagined himself on a small piece of almost unexplored land identifying species of birds, insects and plants.

Stephens Island, or Takapourewa, stands at the far northern tip of Marlborough Province on New Zealand's South Island. Despite being less than four kilometres from the coast, it had long remained untouched owing to the difficulty of accessing it. The lighthouse was erected there in 1891 as a guide to navigation in the turbulent waters of Cook Strait and it was, when it first appeared, the highest and most powerful light in New Zealand.

Lyall settled at the lighthouse with his wife and son in 1893. With them came the cat Tibbles who is, in reality, the main character of this story. The pregnant Tibbles was able to wander freely about the island. Whenever she returned to the lighthouse, she presented her owners with the corpses of a strange kind of bird. Lyall started to take an interest in these curious bodies and, despite his limited knowledge of taxidermy, managed to preserve a few specimens. Unable to identify them, and with the hunch that he was in the presence of an important discovery, he sent a specimen to Walter Buller, a New Zealand ornithologist, who recorded it as a previously undescribed species of wren. The discovery attracted the attention of the ornithological community. Lionel W. Rothschild, the famous British zoologist and banker, requested that a number of specimens be sent to him. The bird was catalogued by Rothschild – not without some controversy – as a new species, *Xenicus lyalli*, belonging to the Passeriforme order. But while the taxonomists were busily working away, back on the island the presence of the birds was dwindling. A suspicion began to form that the growing family of cats – and, perhaps, the activities of some naturalists attempting to secure specimens – were decimating their population. Barely more than a year had passed since then when *The Press*, the Christchurch newspaper, pronounced: *There is very good reason to believe that the bird is no longer to be found on the island, and, as it is not known to exist anywhere else, it has apparently become quite extinct. This is probably a record performance in the way of extermination.*

Before the arrival of Tibbles the cat, no other predatory mammal had ever set foot on the island. In 1899, the new keeper took shots at more than a hundred wild cats, but twenty-six years had to go by before it was possible to declare the island officially feline-free. Lyall was probably one of the very few human beings who saw the bird alive. The behaviour of *Xenicus lyalli* more closely resembled a mouse than a bird: it was nocturnal and unable to fly.

30

Stephens Island Lighthouse

Cook Strait,

Pacific Ocean

Oceania

40° 24′ 00″ S
174° 00′ 00″ E

Date of construction: 1891–94
Date of lighting: 1894
Automated: 1989
Active
Cast-iron tower
Height of tower: 15m
Focal height: 183m
Range: 18 n.m.
Light characteristic: one white flash at
6-second intervals

Stephens Island is hard to reach. The supply of materials and the replacement of keepers was carried out by a derrick that transferred them from boat to land. In 1989, the lighthouse-keepers were withdrawn from service and in 2000 the original light was replaced by a new rotating beacon controlled remotely.

Today, the best-known residents of Stephens are the tuataras. The island is a sanctuary for this rare, almost extinct reptile.

Svyatonossky Lighthouse

ACCORDING TO THE 1875 regulation passed by Tsar Alexander II for the recruitment of lighthouse-keepers in the White Sea, any keeper ought to be familiar with the tough living conditions on the northern coast, they should be competent, well-disciplined, of good moral standing and endowed with the robust health capable of tolerating the challenges of the task. In addition, it was essential that they master the operation of the lighthouse and of the meteorological equipment, as well as possessing elementary knowledge of medicine and hygiene.

AT THE DAWN OF the twentieth century, Bagretsov, the Svyatonossky lighthouse-keeper, lost his sight. First he found difficulties writing in the logbook, later he noticed that he was struggling to make out the ships on the horizon that were changing course from the Barents Sea towards the Holy Nose peninsula, and finally he realized he could barely make out the wicks of the bulbs. But Bagretsov was a tenacious man. Besides, his wife helped him out with the more complicated tasks. And so, far from asking to retire, determined to remain in post, he sent notification of the diminishment of his faculties to the manager of the White Sea lighthouses, Colonel Vasiliev, who, having been most impressed by the excellent operating conditions, assigned him an assistant.

Life in the lighthouse continued as normal until 1913 when Rear Admiral Bukhteev's ship turned up unannounced on the Tersky coast. The news that a blind man was in charge of the Svyatonossky light had reached St Petersburg. A number of opportunists keen to take Bagretsov's place had sent letters to the Hydrographic Service claiming again and again that it was quite impossible to entrust the working of this facility to someone who couldn't see. Bukhteev's unexpected visit was intended to ascertain whether there was any truth to these claims. Following a very thorough inspection, the rear admiral wrote in his report: *Though blind, Bagretsov has a serious commitment to his work and shows great skill in discharging his role. He has a special facility for detecting any anomaly in the functioning of the light or any disturbance in the turning mechanism. With the help of his wife and his assistant who is charged with the meteorological observations, he is capable of adequately managing all matters related to the lighthouse. It is proper that he should be rewarded for so many years of good performance.*

THE BLIND LIGHTHOUSE-KEEPER carried out his work until the start of the Russian Revolution, subsequently passing on the baton to his son. By that time, Nicholas II, the last of the tsars, no longer had the time to deal with the lighthouses of the White Sea.

31

Svyatonossky Lighthouse

BARENTS SEA AND
WHITE SEA

EUROPE

68° 08′ 01″ N
39° 46′ 02″ E

Date of construction: 1862
Date of lighting: 1862
Automated: 2002
Active
Tapered octagonal wooden tower
Height of tower: 22m
Focal height: 94m
Range: 22 n.m.

Following the construction of the Svyatonossky Lighthouse, a head keeper and six assistants were assigned to its upkeep. The conditions of this posting, located above the Arctic Circle, were particularly extreme, and during the first two winters almost the entire team died of scurvy.

However, the lighthouse's final keeper, Mikhail Ivanovich Gorbunov, took on the post in 1966 and managed to keep doing his job for thirty-six years.

БАРЕНЦЕВО МОРЕ

110

113

28

57

38

50

38

44

Svyatonossky

46

62

62

42

52

42

44

46

54

27

19

9

48

45

17

30

27

10

14

БЕЛОЕ
МОРЕ

87

30

87

64

105

82

70

23

48

SVYATOI
NOS

2000 m

OYNOY

KOLSKI POLUÓSTROV

*Ozero
lokangskoye*

Reka lokanga

ROSSÏYA
Россия

Tillamook Rock Lighthouse

ON 18 SEPTEMBER 1879, a boat approaches a basalt islet shaped like a sea-monster, which sticks out of the water a couple of kilometres from the steep Tillamook coast. Travelling on board are John R. Trewavas (a master mason from Portland and an experienced lighthouse-builder) and his assistant, a sailor by the name of Cherry. Trewavas is due to inspect the islet to choose the best position for erecting a lighthouse. But Tillamook Rock will not let itself be conquered easily. In his attempt to reach the rock, Trewavas slips and is dragged away by the swell. Though Cherry throws himself into the water to help, he is unable to rescue him. Trewavas's body was never found.

One year earlier, Congress allocated $50,000 for the construction of a first-rate lighthouse that was intended to facilitate navigation on the rough northern Oregon coast. Nobody at the time could have predicted that the actual cost would end up being double what had been anticipated and include Trewavas's life.

IN TIME, a head lighthouse-keeper and four assistants were charged with over-seeing the operation of Tillamook Rock. Their routine was to remain in post for three months then have two free weeks on land. But the isolation in the small outbuildings, the frequent storms and the constant fog impacted their physical and mental states, and though their working periods at the lighthouse were shortened, there began to be episodes of tension between the keepers.

The first keeper, Albert Roeder, made it through four months before hand-ing in his notice. Some furious bosses communicated with their assistants by passing notes at dinnertime so as to avoid speaking to them. According to a local paper, keeper Bjorlin was removed from service after trying to end the life of his assistant by putting pieces of ground glass in his food. Another assistant was evacuated in August 1906, reported to be suffering from *extreme nervousness* and a possible mental disorder. By now, the lighthouse was known as Terrible Tilly.

SEVENTY-EIGHT YEARS after it began to work, the light at Tillamook Rock goes out; the lighthouse is replaced by a whistle beacon, and the rock passes into private hands. In 1980, it is acquired for $50,000 – curiously the same figure that was assigned a century ago for the building of the lighthouse – by property developer Mimi Morissette, who transforms the place into the Eter-nity at Sea columbarium, a unique store for the ashes of the deceased on the high seas. The project is frozen for legal reasons, but some thirty urns remain in storage in the lighthouse's outbuildings, including those of Morissette's own parents. And perhaps, not too far away, the mortal remains of John Trewavas still lie hidden in the depths of the rock.

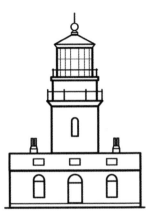

32

Tillamook Rock Lighthouse

Pacific Ocean

North America

45° 56' 15" N
124° 01' 08" W

Date of construction: 1880
Date of lighting: 1881
Deactivated: 1957
Tower of basalt masonry, brick and iron
Height of tower: 19m
Focal height: 41m
Range: 18 n.m.
Original lens: Fresnel, 1st order

A few days before the light came into operation, the vessel *Lupatia*, in the middle of a thick fog, was dragged towards the coast by strong winds. The lighthouse workers heard the sailors' voices and hurried to signal with their lamps. However, the following morning, the lifeless bodies of *Lupatia*'s crew were found on the beaches of Tillamook Head. There was only one survivor: the ship's dog managed to swim to shore.

500 m

23,

16

20

PACIFIC OCEAN

37

20

16

20

10

TILLAMOOK HEAD

23,

20

Bird Point

31

14₆

51

TILLAMOOK
ROCK

40

10₉

27₄

CANNON
BEACH

OREGON
(UNITED STATES)

20

44

33 La Vieille Lighthouse

GORLE BELLA
ROCK,
POINTE DU
RAZ,
PLOGOFF,
FINISTERRE
(FRANCE)

TWO CORSICAN *mutilés de guerre*, disabled ex-servicemen, Mandolini and Ferracci, are assigned the role of assistants at La Vieille, a lighthouse placed on the Gorle Bella – the name coming from Breton, *the most distant rock* – opposite the Pointe du Raz.

Mandolini is afraid of the sea; he has a punctured lung and compromised mobility in one of his arms. Ferracci is living with a bullet lodged in his body and he struggles to climb the one hundred and twenty steps up to the lamp. As soon as they realize that their ill-treated bodies will not be able to tolerate the tough conditions in this isolated place, they ask for a transfer. Their repeated requests, despite being supported by medical reports, are denied.

AT THE END OF the First World War, the French state favoured the reintroduction into work of the numerous people disabled by the conflict. A law of 1924 established a list of reserved occupations intended for these ends, among them park-keepers, postmen and museum guards. The administration also included the role of lighthouse-keeper on the list, presuming, perhaps, that this was only a light sort of task.

IN DECEMBER 1925, the main keeper is on leave and the two Corsican assistants find themselves alone in the lighthouse. It is then that a powerful and protracted storm breaks out over the French coast. Isolated for weeks, exhausted and out of provisions, Mandolini and Ferracci run up the black flag to ask for help. But no help comes; the waves are so intense that no boat can approach.

In the small hours of 19 February 1926, the schooner *Surprise* runs aground on the nearby Plogoff reefs and its eight crew die in the wreck. That night, the lamp at La Vieille had remained unlit, the foghorn had not worked correctly and the black flag was still flying at the lighthouse top.

A week later, Clet Coquet, a local fisherman, guides his boat to the vicinity of the lighthouse. His son Pierre and Nicolas Kerninon – keeper of the Ar-Men Lighthouse – manage to haul themselves along ropes through the turbulent Atlantic waters to reach the rock. There they find the two lighthouse-keepers still alive but *black as devils and their clothes in shreds*.

AFTER THESE EVENTS were given wide press coverage under headlines like *Two Mutilés in Hell*, the role of lighthouse-keeper disappeared from the list of occupations reserved for war veterans of the French Republic.

33

La Vieille Lighthouse

IROISE SEA,
ATLANTIC OCEAN
EUROPE

48° 02′ 26″ N
04° 45′ 23″ W

Date of construction: 1882–87
Date of lighting: 1887
Automated: 1995
Active
Granite tower
Height of tower: 26.9m
Focal height: 33.9m
Range: 15 n.m.
Light characteristic: white, red and green with a group of two eclipses and one eclipse every 12 seconds

Like in other isolated lighthouses in the Iroise Sea – La Jument, Ar-Men and Kéréon – the relief of the keepers and the work of provisioning La Vieille were carried out using a pulley system called a *cartahu*. The lighthouse-keeper had to secure himself to a seat that transported him, suspended, on an acrobatic flight from the boat to the rock or vice versa. The manoeuvre was particularly dangerous owing to the boat's proximity to the rocks, and it required great skill both on the part of the pilot and of the keepers.

Wenwei Zhou Lighthouse

WENWEI ZHOU
OR GAP ROCK,
WANSHAN
ARCHIPELAGO,
HONG KONG
(CHINA)

EVEN BEFORE the nineteenth century, China tea was already in high demand in the British Empire. Although commercial relations between Britain and the Qing dynasty were amicable to begin with, they soon drifted into crisis. The confrontation sparked the first Opium War, at the end of which, in 1842, the defeated Chinese ceded the island of Hong Kong to the British.

TO THE SOUTH OF Hong Kong, like green brushstrokes on the South China Sea, stretches Wanshan, the archipelago of ten thousand islands, vast and mysterious. Around 1850, the growth in sea traffic suggested that some light ought to be thrown onto the waters. The British understood the need to position lighthouses on rocks belonging to the Qing Empire. Thus both governments were compelled to negotiate the building and care of several lighthouses scattered over the islands. One unofficial consequence of this collaboration led to a common practice in the keeping of the Hong Kong lighthouses: most of the keepers were of Eurasian origin, generally the children of British fathers and Chinese mothers. Unconnected to any governmental policies, this was embedded as a tradition of which the lighthouse-keepers became proud.

FORCE 4. FORCE 5. FORCE 6. These are the measurements of a powerful wind lashing a steep rock, separated from the coast by 80 kilometres of aggressive waters and drawn on the map of the Wanshan Archipelago like the tail-tip of a mosquito that has come to rest on the sea. A stone islet fractured into two parts, which the Chinese call Wenwei Zhou, and the British, Gap Rock.

ON ITS HIGHER PORTION, the southern one, stands a tower that looks like a castle. In 1892, a lamp was brought from Sweden to illuminate the seas of Asia with Scandinavian brilliance. In the eyes of those who built it, this fortress seemed invincible, but just a few years later, a typhoon left the lighthouse mutilated. The authorities travelled over to assess the damage, but since Wenwei Zhou has no harbour and it is not easy to clamber onto, a wave hurled the visitors into the water. It wasn't until they managed to repair the lighthouse that somebody realized that it had been erected in an unsuitable location. The northern part of the rock was safer when it came to hurricanes.

But while storms didn't manage to put the light out, wars did. Leftover pieces of shrapnel and holes in the walls provide evidence of intense fighting on Wenwei Zhou during the Chinese Civil War (1927–49). Following this conflict, the lighthouse remained unlit for forty years, until it was repaired in the 1980s. Today it is an automated lamp that signals to craft navigating south of China, reporting the presence of the tiny Mosquito Island.

34

**Wenwei Zhou
Lighthouse**

SOUTH CHINA SEA,
PACIFIC OCEAN
ASIA

21° 45′ 50″ N
113° 56′ 16″ E

Date of construction: 1890–92
Date of lighting: 1892
Deactivated: between 1927 and 1949
Automated and reactivated: 1986
Active
Brick and cement tower
Height of tower: 24m
Focal height: 45m
Range: 20 n.m.
Original lens: 1st order

A travel agency in Zhuhai (Guangdong
Province, China) tried to make the
lighthouse into a tourist destination.
They offered excursions for small
groups to travel by boat to Wenwei
Zhou and spend a night on the island.
After several unsuccessful attempts
at these journeys, the idea was
abandoned.

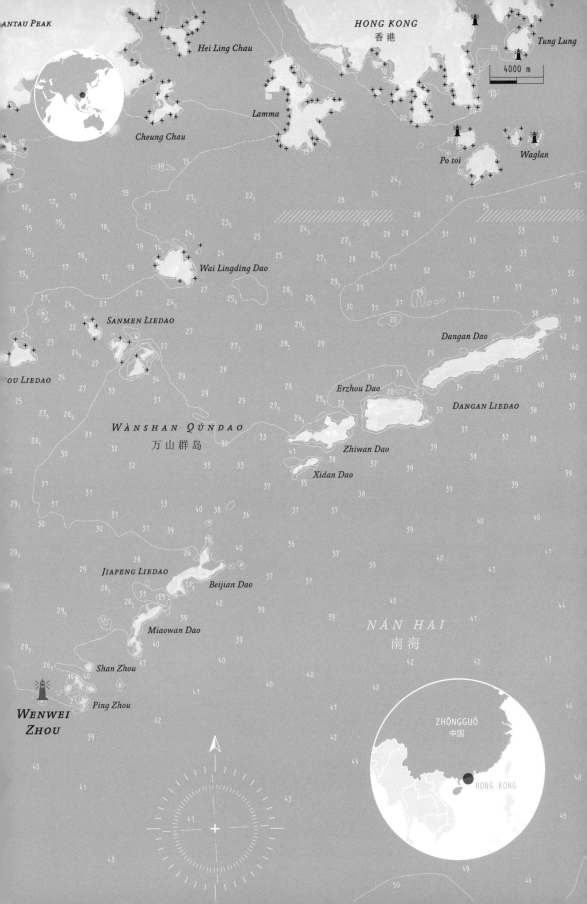

THIS BOOK IS DEDICATED
TO THOSE WHO ONCE SERVED ON
AN ISOLATED LIGHTHOUSE
AND TO THE PEOPLE WHO HAVE
CONTRIBUTED TO COLLECTING AND
PASSING ON THEIR STORIES.

Jose Luis González Macías is a Spanish writer, graphic designer and publisher. In 2003 he published several short stories and poems which received the Letras Jóvenes award. Soon after he became interested in graphic design and, since then, has worked for museums and cultural institutions designing books and other graphic material. Along with Lia Peinador, he runs Ediciones Menguantes, a small publishing house based in León in northern Spain. A fan of maps since he was a child, in *A Brief Atlas of the Lighthouses at the End of the World* he has combined his passion for words and images in more than thirty stories about remote lighthouses.

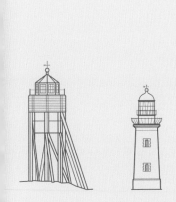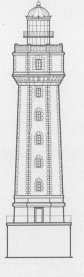